Sacred Journey Vol. II

Exploring the Mystery of the Godhead.
Revealing the Shema: Father, Son – Messiah and Holy Spirit

Rev John K Cairns Jr, D.Min.

Sacred Journey II is a companion to Sacred Journey I. Both are Hebraically Interpretive and Expositional Apologetics on Fundamental Biblical Beliefs

TABLE OF CONTENTS

About the Author & Dedication.....................4

Recommendation & Thanks 5

Preface... 6

Introduction...8

I   The Godhead....................................12

II The Godhead: Hidden Discovery..........17

III The Godhead: What do we
     discover?...25

IV The Godhead: Seeking Non-Verbal
     Revelation..38

V   The Godhead: Verbal Revelation..........49

VI The Godhead: The Shema and the
     Trinity..53

VII The Godhead: Father.........................68

VIII The Godhead: Son – Jesus..................80

IX The Godhead: Son – Messiah...............94

X	The Godhead: Messiah - Son of God and Son of Man............................105
XI	The Godhead: Messiah – Word, Logos and Wisdom..........................119
XII	The Godhead: Messiah – Immanuel.....................................133
XIII	The Godhead: The Holy Spirit............148
XIV	Closing Thoughts............................165

Finding Salvation on the Roman Road......168

Endnotes...170

About the Author:

John K. Cairns Jr. is a third-generation ordained minister. He received a B.A. from the College of New Jersey, an M.A. in Biblical Languages O.T. from The Assemblies of God Theological Seminary (Springfield, MO.) and a D.Min. in Messianic Jewish Leadership from The King's University (Dallas Texas). He serves as Senior Pastor at Capital Assembly of God (Hamilton, NJ) since 1991, and assists Metro-Jewish Resources in their Educational studies and teaches at the N.J. School of Ministry (Assemblies of God).

Dedication

To my wife Ginny, children Carla, Jacqueline, Julie and John. You have been with me the better part of my life and have enriched my journey greatly because of it! Love You!

Recommendation: Barri Cae Seif, Ph.D.

- "Do yourself a favor. Please read, devour and enjoy Reverend Dr. Jack Cairns new book. He indulges the reader to go deep into God's word. Rev. Cairns beautifully weaves Hebrew into his insights, illuminating deep things of the Holy Spirit, the Ruach HaKodesh, for the reader. Your spirit will be encouraged and strengthened."

Special Thanks

To Marguerite Oswald for your many hours of work editing the text and smoothing out some roughly hewn thoughts.

All scripture is from the New International Version unless otherwise noted.
Cover Art: Ramon Ocasio 2020

Preface

For whom is this book intended?

Are you curious about the mysteries of the Godhead? Have you felt ill-equipped to explain or defend some deep truths about the Godhead? Then this book is intended for you. This small volume contains *uncommon knowledge* about the mysteries of the Godhead. New knowledge? Not new, but *recovered* knowledge!

My purpose for this volume originates in a personal desire to restore re-discovered truths about the Godhead drawn from ancient interpretive understandings of scripture, especially those concerning Messiah. It is a book for those who want more concrete evidence to support their own beliefs and provide a strong defense for the foundations of their Biblical faith.

If you have had doubts about the constancy and unity of truth to be found within the Old and New Testaments concerning the Godhead and other related truths, this book is for you.

If you are a Bible teacher and are looking for a clear way of presenting the Godhead to your students, this book is for you.

If you have yet to be introduced to or convinced of this truth statement: *'The Old Testament is the foundation for all of Jesus' and His Disciples' theology'*, then this book is for you.

Modern Biblical Study is about 'recovery and reclamation' as much as it is about 'revelation'. Some especially important methods of interpretation that are demonstrated within scripture, along with reclaimed and well-established interpretations, had been forgotten and therefore neglected.

This volume does not make a claim to have recovered everything, but it makes a sincere attempt to share what has been rediscovered by both Jewish and Gentile believers.

Introduction

Why is the Godhead a mystery and in need of being revealed?

If there is a mystery surrounding the Godhead, it is because of a loss of Biblical knowledge that was never intended to be forgotten. What is needed in our time is for our Biblical revelation and understanding of the Godhead to be rediscovered and reclaimed!

By whom? By modern Christians, Messianic Jews (believers in Jesus) and those who practice all forms of Judaism. Why? Because after some nineteen hundred years, since the last book of the canonized New Testament was written, we have left behind, by mixture of accident and purpose, interpreted understandings of the revelations of Scripture concerning the Godhead that were once the mainstream (or majority view) teachings of the Judeans at the time of Jesus' advent.

What caused such a departure from these well-established beliefs? There are many reasons, but primarily the faith-partitioning that occurred between those who followed Jesus as the Messiah and those (primarily Jews) who did not. For a clearer understanding of the reasons and ways in which this partitioning occurred, I recommend Daniel Boyarin's book "Border Lines, The Partition of Judeo-Christianity", University of Pennsylvania Press, 2004.

Some may discover the following to be a new understanding "that what we now call Christianity was once a fast-growing sect within the faith of the ancient Judeans of the Second Temple Period. It took over a few hundred years for a Gentile-focused Christianity and a Jewish-focused Rabbinical Judaism to arise through the separation from each other. This was accomplished by formulating doctrines and practices which made them distinct from one another."

These separate doctrines took form as both groups used methods of interpretation that emphasized these distinctions. Unfortunately, it was not just what they held onto but what they let go of as well that divided them.

Which group lost the most during this partitioning? Today, few on either side would admit to any real loss by the shifting or editing of beliefs but, each has sacrificed certain positions over time. The Jewish people should benefit from a re-examination of what they once believed, and the Christians would benefit from a re-examination of when and where their beliefs were first established.

I fall into the Jesus group since the acceptance or rejection of Jesus as God and Messiah are the most important distinctions held between all forms of Christianity and all forms of Judaism. It would be fair to say that every other point of separation between us is attached to this primary belief.

Though there are points of belief that are of lesser distinction, they are still of great importance and should be considered relevant when speaking about our differences. But this book does not intend to speak of all such distinctions.

This book hopes to re-discover what were once the belief<u>s</u> held by the majority about the Godhead within both camps and might surprise both Christians and Jews. It is my genuine hope that both sides would reclaim these interpretive truths, reframe the history of our collective faith, and correct our doctrinal narratives.

Owning the truth about our once mutually held beliefs should be a mutually held objective. By accepting that many of our beliefs were once held in common, we will strengthen the resolve to trust our own faith, further assisting us in defending our faith as it supports our witness. Our hope is that our Jewish friends will take these truths to heart and by finding common ground will make room to reconsider their historic views on Jesus and Messiah.

NOTE: 'Rabbinical Judaism' refers very broadly to a form of Judaism that came into existence following the destruction of the Temple in 70 C.E. (Common Era). Beginning as a small sect, it took many centuries to unify the Jewish people around centralized Rabbinic and Talmudic interpretations of faith and practice. Originally influenced by Pharisaic rabbis who put the Oral Law into writing within the 2nd Century C.E., Rabbis strongly relied upon this formative work to build a defense against the increasing acceptance of Jesus as Messiah by the Jewish people in the first few centuries of the Common Era.

I

The Godhead

As we approach the topic of the Godhead, we approach the very heart of theological and interpretive discovery. Is this a new discovery? No! "The existence of God, for the biblical writers, was ever present and assumed." As G. K. Chestertown rightly observed, "God is not the chief character in the Bible; He is its only character." [1.]

We who are on a Sacred Journey are constantly engaged in a dialogue with others who are on this journey with us. We speak about beliefs we hold in common concerning God. We have already spoken about the faith that is exercised in our walk, and it might be good to speak about what is meant when we use the word 'faith' in correspondence to our following the God of the Bible.

"Historically, when the Bible uses the word *'emunah'* (faith) for man's relationship to God, it always denotes, not just a belief, but a "trust" in God. This faith did not involve a hope that God does exist, it was the simple acceptance that God did exist. Faith is an emotional and responsive term rather than a cerebral or cognitive term. 'Cognitive' means to draw conclusions brought about through ordered thought. Faith to the ancient Israelite was synonymous with *'bittakon'* (trust), rather than with God's reality and existence." [2.]

In the time of the biblical Israelites, hardly anyone doubted that God existed. Theoretical atheism was virtually unknown. All the tensions in the matter of faith were with regard to man's relationship with God, that is, whether man conducts himself adequately in the presence of the Being who makes moral and religious demands upon him. The believer acts in such a manner that, to him, God is real.

It is no accident that *'emunah'* is applied to other human beings, as well as to God. It makes no sense to speak of belief in the existence of one's neighbor, except by a famed and foreign sophistication to ancient thought. It is impossible to deny that the neighbor exists, but it does not follow necessarily from the neighbor's existence that he is trustworthy. 3.

How does trust relate to the Godhead and scriptural revelation? Trust and confidence can be seen as the two faces of faith. In all matters of faith, trust and confidence are the two necessary responses of the believer that makes their faith come alive. As we shared previously, faith is the evidence of things unseen, meaning the things of God, and the evidence is marked by trust and confidence in the one in whom we place our faith.

In our ancient biblical past, trust and confidence were the hallmarks of a true believer in God. This included the patriarchs, the prophets of God, kings and queens, soldiers, shepherds, priests, husbands, wives, children, slaves and every other manner of living situation, revealed their faith by the trust and confidence they placed in their God. In the Bible there may have been arguments over who was the real God, but there were never arguments made that God did not exist. *The existence of God was not a subject undertaken by any of the writers of the Bible.* 4.

Arguments were given concerning how to recognize the one true God but never for the existence of God, which may be why we as believers today find it challenging to prove the existence of God by using the Scriptures as evidence. Man is the one who takes it upon himself to prove or disprove the existence of God. And God does not seem to make it a priority to prove His existence. He just simply IS!

Even when God takes the opportunity to reveal Himself, He does not seem to make much of an effort to prove He exists. He just declares that He does. God's approach to revelation concerning Himself, is a manner in which He is always partially hidden, never fully unveiled, and never answering all of our questions pertaining to His being God. I am sure it matters to Him that we believe that He is God, but He seems content in the truth that our knowledge of Him must involve faith over proven fact.

What I mean by 'faith over fact' is that God makes the best impression upon us in 'spirit' more so than in natural functions. What we might want is for God to be encountered in the 'natural realm' of His creation. We want our eyes to see Him, our hands to touch Him, our ears to hear His voice, and yet He seems more inclined to encourage our faith and not to be the process of our works.

The Godhead is to always be understood as existing as spirit and not flesh. This does not negate the revelation of the incarnate God Messiah, but let us be honest, in the more than 6000-year history of the Bible, the revelation of the God-in-flesh was but just a brief moment in time; and what a moment it was. But it was still within time; it was barely a moment!

As we look to comprehend the revelation of the Godhead, as shared with us in Scripture, we see that God, while interacting in the lives of men throughout history, chooses to remain in 'spirit. This world, which is the creation of God, is the arena of men, it is not where God dwells. God does not dwell in the natural, for that is not His true self. He is 'supernatural spirit'.

II

The Godhead:
Hidden Discovery

God's "hiddenness" has become the number one issue for individuals who believe that they are rational thinkers. They may consider it more of a problem than an issue. But for us, as believers, it is an issue and not a major one. It certainly is not a new issue because we see it evidenced in the doubts that Thomas expressed following the death of Jesus.

This issue, in more modern times, does not cast a doubt that someone was raised to life, but that that someone was indeed God.

Beginning in the Middle Ages, individuals began to look for verifiable proof that God existed. Since they were not alive at the time of the Gospels, and the Scriptures themselves did not prove the existence of God to their satisfaction, their call for proof led them away from mere faith to philosophical or ontological arguments.

However, these arguments were never satisfactory. Proof was still eluding them, and it led to their throwing up their hands and saying that one simply must take a "leap of faith" as Soren Kierkegaard concludes. It appears we are driven back to a position of faith whether we like it or not. And it does appear that God is not interested in changing that reality.

It does not mean that believing in God through the exercising of one's faith is unreasonable. I believe that the use of reason strengthens one's faith. Atheism, to me, is unreasonable. Darwin's theory of evolution is unreasonable to me. To not believe that there are absolute truths that support and uphold the universe around us is unreasonable to me.

> Isaiah 1:18   18 "Come now, let us reason together," says the LORD.

The belief that there is a God is not unreasonable. In fact, reasoning becomes a major bulwark as an approach used to discover

God and strengthening our belief in His existence.

Not all roads lead to God and not all paths or methods of discovery lead to God. You may wish to make a pumpkin pie. But if you choose to make it without pumpkin, or you decide that you will freeze the mixture instead of baking it, or that you will use some liquid other than milk, you will end up with something, but your friends won't recognize it as pumpkin pie.

Part of the reasoning process is to accept that there are certain parameters that guide us to wise and truthful conclusions. It is God who chooses the path. God who establishes the borderlines. God who is the author of the kind of faith man needs to be able to discover and encounter Him. While He appears to place limitations upon His encounters within the natural realm, which we feel could be used to prove His existence, He does not place any limitations upon our ability or opportunity to encounter Him or prove Him by faith.

We also must accept that, for believers, our faith must travel back two-thousand years to engage the stories of the incarnate God who walked this earth. Acceptance of these stories as truth still requires faith on our part. Regardless of what we do, we will always need to exercise our faith to believe and trust that the stories we are reading are true. We live our lives with confidence that this is a reasonable faith, and that we have all the proof we need that our God lives.

Hidden Discovery

If God remains hidden in His supernatural state of being, how can we discover who He is? This becomes the most important priority for us as we interpret the content of Biblical Scripture. Our task is not to interpretively prove that God exists, for scripture readily assumes that He does, but our task is to reveal '**Who**' God is. The Scriptures now become the most important set of documents ever produced because they are the only infallible documents we can put our trust in that reveals to mankind the state of being, personhood, character and nature of the one true God.

The discovery of God begins the moment we open the Bible and begin to read. It might have been nice if God would have constructed and written the Bible topically. For instance, instead of Genesis beginning as it does with two unique composed chapters on the creation of the universe and mankind, we would have preferred that he wrote an exposé about who He is, which would hopefully include His origin. We would appreciate it if He would take the time to explain His source of knowledge and power in a way that would help to settle the debate about His nature.

We would have Him move on to Chapter 2 and really explain the origins of the universe and whether or not the universe is billions of years old or just 6,000 to 7,000 years old. Chapter 3 could be about mankind and what God really expects of him. Another chapter could be about the laws of God, gathering all of them into one place having them outlined in priority of their importance, and He could explain exactly how these laws benefit mankind.

Next, He could write chapters about community, male and female relationships, child-rearing, healing, the problem of pain, the governance of man, worship and religious practices, and just about anything else we would like God to speak on. For us, we would require the Bible to be more of an operator's manual for life, complete with inset tabs and keyword references at the back. Our Bible would not end with the book of Revelation but with a group of all-inclusive creeds to extinguish all such debates over how we are to properly apply the wisdom of the Book. But this is not how God designed the Bible.

If we are to discover the Godhead, and all its corresponding attributes, we must begin by reading the Bible with an intent placed upon such discovery. If we want to discover the truth concerning the Godhead, then we must sincerely purpose to do so.

While reading, when we come upon a word or a connotation of the name or names of God, or we read about an encounter someone has with God, or read about instructions or requirements for how men are to follow Him that are obviously coming from God, or there seems to be some kind of natural or supernatural appearing of the Godhead on earth, or we read prophecies given by men and women that are meant to declare things that are yet to come and which God has ordained to happen, we should pay attention and record all of these revelations.

We compile what God has shared about Himself and begin to piece each individual truth together forming a collected Revelation of God. It may be easier in some way to merely extrapolate from the page bits of information that in context are related to the God who is now revealing himself. However, the revelations that we are becoming aware of are deeply rooted in the supernatural realm, much more so than in the natural world around us. And so, while the concepts may be easily spotted on the page, their meaning and interconnectedness can often leave us strangely baffled and yet totally inspired.

III

The Godhead:

What do we Discover?

Where should we start in our discovery of the revelations embedded within scripture on the Godhead? We could begin with the book of Genesis and it would be a fascinating study for after all it does start with "in the beginning." I don't believe though that we are required to move chronologically from the first verse of Scripture to the last because it didn't seem so important to God to reveal Himself in such a manner, therefore I don't believe that we are bound to that approach. I would like it if we first examined some of the attributes of God and in so doing it should inform and direct our further interpretive study.

When we speak conceptually about God, we are referencing a Being that is highly exalted and supreme and totally different than any of His creation. The ancient Judeans of the biblical era, Rabbinical Judaism and the modern church hold this to be true about the God of the Bible. "Since by definition, belief in God is belief in the unique being totally different from any of his creations, the problem for Jewish, as for all theists (sic. which includes Christians), has always been how to give expression in language to the nature of that deity." **5.**

> Deuteronomy 4:35   35 "You were shown these things so that you might know that the LORD is God; besides him there is no other."
>
> Isaiah 46:9   9 "Remember the former things, those of long ago; I am God, and there is no other; I am God, and there is none like me."

"The Bible abounds in descriptions of God in human terms. He has an eye and a hand; He is good, compassionate, and merciful; His wrath is kindled against evildoers; He occasionally changes His mind and yet everywhere it is stated that He is not a human being who can change His mind." **6.**

That we are not God and that He is totally other than who we are becomes obvious to even the most casual reader of Scripture. And it is this revelation that can cause the reader to become extremely humbled and move them to a place of inspired worship and awe, which would be an appropriate response. Too often, this understanding of God is read with a heart that takes offence because of the apparent inadequacies we see within ourselves, giving form to a narcissistic jealousy that rises up within us.

If we are to move forward in our discovery of the Godhead, we will need to choose which one of these two responses to revelation we will take. Only the first one will move us closer in our relationship with Him and my hope is that it will be your choice as well.

"Finally, in order to enrich our knowledge of the nature of God, for what greater object of thought and study exist than He?" [7.]

As we continue our study of the Godhead, we find ourselves in strong agreement with Hebrew Christian, Myer Pearlman, that we are attempting the greatest object of thought of all the sciences, all the philosophies, and all the theologies in our quest to know God by means of interpretive discovery. Our quest begins and ends with what the scriptures reveal about God.

For us, our study began with discovering one of the attributes of God. In the last chapter we discerned that when we speak conceptually about the attributes of God, we are referencing a Being that is highly exalted and supreme, and 'totally different from any of His creation', meaning His attributes are wholly other. [8.]

We previously discovered that God, in essence exists as a non-spatial Spirit; He is always present (omnipresent).

> Psalm 139:7-10 [7] "Where can I go from your Spirit? Where can I flee from your presence? [8] If I go up to the heavens, you are there; if I make my bed in the depths, you are there. [9] If I rise on the wings of the dawn, if I settle on the far side of the sea, [10] even there your hand will guide me, your right hand will hold me fast."

God dwells among all of His creation but especially *in the inner-most being of man.*

> Isaiah 57:15 15 For this is what the high and lofty One says-- he who lives forever, whose name is holy: "I live in a high and holy place, but also with him who is contrite and lowly in spirit, to revive the spirit of the lowly and to revive the heart of the contrite."

God has no beginning, and He has no end; He is immortal.

> 1 Timothy 1:17 "Now to the King eternal, immortal, invisible, the only God, be honor and glory for ever and ever. Amen."

> 1 Timothy 6:16 "who alone is immortal and who lives in unapproachable light, whom no one has seen or can see. To him be honor and might forever. Amen."

God cannot be ruled or controlled by others but He Himself controls all things; He is All-powerful (omnipotent).

> Isaiah 40:10 10 "See, the Sovereign LORD comes with power, and his arm rules for

him. See, his reward is with him, and his recompense accompanies him."

Isaiah 46:5 "To whom will you compare me or count me equal? To whom will you liken me that we may be compared?"

Isaiah 45:5 "I am the LORD, and there is no other; apart from me there is no God. I will strengthen you, though you have not acknowledged me,"

God is all-knowing (omniscient).

Isaiah 40:28 28 "Do you not know? Have you not heard? The LORD is the everlasting God, the Creator of the ends of the earth. He will not grow tired or weary, and his understanding no one can fathom."

Acts 15:8 8 "God, who knows the heart, showed that he accepted them by giving the Holy Spirit to them, just as he did to us."

Romans 8:27-28 27 "And he who searches our hearts knows the mind of the Spirit, because the Spirit intercedes for the saints in accordance with God's will. ²⁸ And we know that in all things God works for the good of those who love him, who have been called according to his purpose."

God is wise (wisdom).

> Psalm 104:24   ²⁴ "How many are your works, O LORD! In wisdom you made them all;"

> Proverbs 3:19   ¹⁹ "By wisdom the LORD laid the earth's foundations, by understanding he set the heavens in place;"

God is Loving.

> Exodus 15:13   ¹³ "In your unfailing love you will lead the people you have redeemed. In your strength you will guide them to your holy dwelling."

> Exodus 20:6   ⁶ "but showing love to a thousand *generations* of those who love me and keep my commandments."

Psalm 57:10 [10] "For great is your love, reaching to the heavens; your faithfulness reaches to the skies."

Psalm 136:1-26

[1] "Give thanks to the LORD, for he is good. His love endures forever.

[2] Give thanks to the God of gods. His love endures forever.

[3] Give thanks to the Lord of lords: His love endures forever.

[4] to him who alone does great wonders, His love endures forever.

[5] who by his understanding made the heavens, His love endures forever.

[6] who spread out the earth upon the waters, His love endures forever.

[7] who made the great lights-- His love endures forever.

[8] the sun to govern the day, His love endures forever.

⁹ the moon and stars to govern the night; His love endures forever.

¹⁰ to him who struck down the firstborn of Egypt His love endures forever.

¹¹ and brought Israel out from among them His love endures forever.

¹² with a mighty hand and outstretched arm; His love endures forever.

¹³ to him who divided the Red Sea asunder His love endures forever.

¹⁴ and brought Israel through the midst of it, His love endures forever.

¹⁵ but swept Pharaoh and his army into the Red Sea; His love endures forever.

¹⁶ to him who led his people through the desert, His love endures forever.

¹⁷ who struck down great kings, His love endures forever.

¹⁸ and killed mighty kings-- His love endures forever.

¹⁹ Sihon king of the Amorites His love endures forever.

²⁰ and Og king of Bashan-- His love endures forever.

²¹ and gave their land as an inheritance, His love endures forever.

²² an inheritance to his servant Israel; His love endures forever.

²³ to the One who remembered us in our low estate His love endures forever.

²⁴ and freed us from our enemies, His love endures forever.

²⁵ and who gives food to every creature. His love endures forever.

²⁶ Give thanks to the God of heaven. His love endures forever."

It is important to keep in mind that while we are speaking of the attributes of God, we don't do so in a very nonchalant, passively general or overly familiar way. For while we are able to use our language to define or describe God, we need to be mindful of the fact that our words and our definitions, which hopefully are somewhat accurate, are in no way exhaustive. While our words are necessary and relevant, we must be careful that they don't become irreverent.

It is a much easier task for us to look into, and speak about, the manifest works of God because they can be perceived naturally. But his essence, character and nature are the things that are only supernaturally perceived and are therefore considered 'set apart' or 'holy'. And it is the holy things of God that must be treated with utmost humility and respect. And we sincerely and honestly confess that they are the worthiest and most transforming to our own souls.

Judah Halevi observes that humans can dwell upon God's works but must refrain from describing His nature, "For if we were able to grasp it [His nature] this would be a defect in Him" (Kuzari, 5, 21). [9.] While this may seem a little extreme to our sense of what is cautious and honoring, what Judah is implying is that

God's nature is really beyond our intellectual grasp. If we were to say that we now fully know God, He would no longer be God. As previously cited in Chapter V, "Joseph Albo tells of the Sage who, when invited to describe God's essence, replied: "if I knew Him I would be He" (Sefer ha-Ikkarim 2, 30)." [10.]

"The Jews have always taken the study of the nature of God and our subsequent 'God-talk' seriously. "Consequently, throughout the history of Jewish thought there has been considerable tension in the matter of God talk. To say too much, without qualification, is to fall into the trap of gross anthropomorphism (describing God using human based descriptions: eyes, hands, etc.). To say too little is to court the opposite risk of having so many reservations that the whole concept suffers. Between these extremes Jewish thinkers can be divided into those who passionately declare that, for all the tremendous divide between God and man, God can still be spoken of, within limits, in human terms, and those who prefer the negative path, seeing the sheer wondrousness of God in that he is utterly beyond all human conceptualizations. These latter echo the words of the psalmist (in the usual rendering of the verse): "for Thee silence is praise, O God" (Psalm 62:2)". [11]

So, with little concern that we have attempted to say too much we readily admit that we have not been entirely exhaustive, because we have actually said very little, we close out this chapter.

IV

The Godhead:
Seeking Non-Verbal Revelation

Psalm 8:3-4   3 "When I consider your heavens, the work of your fingers, the moon and the stars, which you have set in place, 4 what is man that you are mindful of him, the son of man that you care for him?"

Psalm 19:1 "For the director of music. A psalm of David. The heavens declare the glory of God; the skies proclaim the work of his hands. 2 Day after day they pour forth speech; night after night they display knowledge. 3 There is no speech or language where their voice is not heard. 4 Their voice goes out into all the earth, their words to the ends of the world. In the heavens he has pitched a tent for the sun, 5 which is like a bridegroom coming forth from his pavilion, like a champion rejoicing to run his course. 6 It rises at one end of the heavens and makes its circuit to the other; nothing is hidden from its heat."

Romans 1:17-22 [17] "For in the gospel a righteousness from God is revealed, a righteousness that is by faith from first to last, just as it is written: "The righteous will live by faith." [Hab 2:4] [18] The wrath of God is being revealed from heaven against all the godlessness and wickedness of men who suppress the truth by their wickedness, [19] since what may be known about God is plain to them, because God has made it plain to them. [20] For since the creation of the world God's invisible qualities-- his eternal power and divine nature-- have been clearly seen, being understood from what has been made, so that men are without excuse. [21] For although they knew God, they neither glorified him as God nor gave thanks to him, but their thinking became futile and their foolish hearts were darkened. [22] Although they claimed to be wise, they became fools."

Non-Verbal Revelation

While there are quite a number of similarities between Christianity and modern Judaism, we do recognize that we also have our differences;

with those differences, perhaps unfortunately, becoming the majority of the things we focus upon. We must be honest by pointing out that some of those differences are not minor in importance as they, very much so, form the distinct and foundational doctrines of our faiths.

Christianity and Judaism both believe in a God who is eternally self-existent. A God who is all-knowing, all-powerful and eternal. Summarily, while both Christians and Jews will primarily use Scripture to verify their statements about God, it should be pointed out that these characteristics of God mentioned above are also able to be discovered or discerned philosophically and scientifically by observing and studying the world around us. "This revelation about God does not consist of words - it is *nonverbal revelation*. The heavens, therefore, offer a silent continual testimony to God." [12].

We will be intellectually honest and say that non-verbal revelation is extremely limited in its scope, but it doesn't take a theologian to come to those conclusions. By merely examining the universe around us the individual is able to admit that there is a God behind everything. They may not call him God. They might say "a great mind", an intellectual force or the unmoved mover, but if that is as deep as their inquiry goes, while it is not blasphemy or heresy, it is just far too simplistic.

It does not take a genius only a discerning intellectual inquiry to perceive the fact that behind the universe there is an all-knowing, all powerful eternal force! That, however, is just the beginning of our probe into discovering and understanding the **who** behind creation.

I want to share a story about an individual that I offer up as evidence of someone who reportedly, by way of mere intellectual inquiry, moved from atheism to a form of "deism." His name is Professor Anthony Flew.

"Antony Flew was the son of a Methodist minister and as a young boy was educated at a Christian boarding school. As a teenager, he decided that the traditional Christian concept of a good God was inconsistent with the presence of evil in the world and thus he adopted atheism. After service in the Royal Air Force during World War II, Flew went on to study philosophy at St. John's College, Oxford, where his teacher was the English linguistic philosopher Gilbert Ryle.

At Oxford, Flew was particularly influenced by critiques of traditional arguments for the existence of God and other religious phenomena by the 18th-century Scottish philosopher David Hume. Flew received a master's degree in 1949 and stayed on at Oxford to teach. He subsequently lectured at the University of Aberdeen, Keele University, and the University of Reading, retiring from the latter in 1982.

In 2004 Flew courted controversy with his announcement that, upon reviewing the scientific evidence, he had come to accept a very limited form of deism, a theological perspective based on the concept of a God who created the world but does not make His will known.

In 1950 Flew delivered a short paper, "Theology and Falsification," before Oxford's Socratic Club (a salon [*club*] then presided over by the well-known Christian apologist C.S. Lewis*). Flew argued that theological utterances about God's nature, presence, power, or goodness are meaningless because there is no conceivable evidence that would refute them. Flew quickly became a prominent figure in the philosophy of religion and popular intellectual spokesperson for atheism. Books by Flew, such as *God and Philosophy* (1966; reissued 2005) and *Atheistic Humanism* (1993).

Flew also provided articulate expositions of atheistic principles that won a wide popular as well as academic following. Flew's writings influenced later atheists, such as Richard Dawkins and Sam Harris, who write for popular as well as academic audiences.

Flew nevertheless maintained an intellectual interest in religion, reading broadly and holding discussions with philosophers and scientists who were also practicing Christians or Jews—particularly the American evangelical philosopher Gary Habermas and the U.S.-

born Jewish scientist Gerald Schroeder.. Flew nevertheless maintained an intellectual interest in religion, reading broadly and holding discussions with philosophers and scientists who were also practicing Christians and Jews.

His announcement drew praise from many Evangelicals and criticism from atheists, many of whom suggested that Flew—in his early 80s and suffering from aphasia—may have been confused or even taken advantage of by individuals with ulterior motives. Flew publicly defended his perspective with the claim that the God he had come to believe in was similar to the "unmoved mover" proposed by Aristotle. However, Flew never [fully] returned to Christianity and continued to deny the survival of the human mind after biological death.

NOTE: Much of Flew's refusal to fully embrace Christianity had to do with his understanding, or what I saw as his lack of understanding, of eternal life for the believer. He was put off by the idea of eternal judgment, which for all of us is not a pleasant understanding of the judgment awaiting those who reject the God of Scripture and his Messiah. But it was really his total misunderstanding of how richly rewarding and fulfilling eternal life in the presence of God would be.

In 2006 Flew was among the signatories of a letter urging British Prime Minister Tony Blair to introduce intelligent design (ID) into science classes in state-supported schools. The 2007 book *There Is a God: How the World's Most Notorious Atheist Changed His Mind*, cowritten by Flew and the Christian author Roy Abraham Varghese, further incensed atheist critics, particularly when it was revealed that Varghese and a ghostwriter did most of the writing." [13.]

NOTE: Let me insert a comment regarding that last statement which infers that Roy Abraham Varghese wrote without Anthony Flew's direct oversight and approval. There is no evidence whatsoever that Varghese may have written something that Flew was not in full agreement with or that it disagreed with Flew's intellectual position on God.

And now, before drawing some conclusions that I personally want to share, I would like to provide some additional background on the "Socratic Club" that was briefly referenced. "From the Oxford University's website: "The Socratic Club is one of Oxford's foremost non-sports clubs. Oxford Pastorate [i.e. chaplaincy] member and club founder, Stella Adwinkle, stated that its purpose would be to provide 'an open forum for the discussion of the intellectual difficulties connected with religion and with Christianity in particular' (Socratic Digest, first issue). Its first president was none other than C. S. Lewis! The subject of the first meeting (held in 1942) was, 'Can Science Render Religion Unnecessary?' Other subjects have been: 'Did the Resurrection Happen?' (1947) and "Theology and Verification" (1950). The original club disbanded in 1972, but new Socratic Clubs have since been formed on the campuses of many American universities." [14].

"Socrates, C.S. Lewis comments, had exhorted men to "follow the argument wherever it led them.""" Antony Flew also held to this principle of inquiry. As he (Lewis) envisioned it, the

Socratic Club was created to apply this principle to one particular subject-- the *pros* and *cons* of the Christian Religion. But make no mistake about it CS Lewis's role as a defender of the faith was without question. For thirteen years running, from 1942 to 1954, C.S. Lewis presided as the club's president. Meetings were held every Monday evening during each of the three academic terms, and unless he was ill or had some other engagement which he was unable to get out of, he was there." [15.]

It is also of interest to note that C.S. Lewis, at approximately the same time, was also engaged in doing live on the air broadcast talks for the BBC. Beginning on August 6, 1941 through April 4, 1944 and taking only one year off (1943), Lewis was asked to give talks on the Christian faith to encourage fellow embattled British citizens; 29 broadcasts in all. Some of the topics were "Scientific Law and Moral Law", "Materialism or Religion", and even one of the targets of these current Spiritual Journey chapters, "God in Three Persons". The texts of these broadcasts were the genesis and basic content of the book many have heard of and read entitled "Mere Christianity" (1952). [16]

V

The Godhead: Verbal Revelation

What we have dealt with so far is a purely intellectual inquiry into subject matter that includes the Godhead from a merely philosophical or scientific viewpoint from observational inquiry. This viewpoint admits that their conclusions are drawn from a source originating in the minds of men as they ask questions of the known universe which is a non-verbal source.

By non-verbal we mean that the source for their evidence is the natural world, and through observation they draw conclusions to determine if there is any evidence of divine activity. Yes, their conclusions are written down and transferred by language and literature, but their original sources do not come from a literary or verbal source.

These writings are therefore limited and have no insightful value to impart through scientific discovery to make claims that there is a God who is knowable or **a God who is personal and desires to form a relationship with His created beings.** The literature produced by those mentioned studies come from departments other than theology. We have already admitted that that form of discovery of the Godhead is extremely limited. Their argument is valid that by only observing the universe we are not capable of proving or even knowing if God is reaching out and perhaps trying to communicate with His creation. For some, like Antony Flew, they would conclude that there is a lack of empirical or scientific evidence that God is interested or even capable of having a relationship with man. But this shows Flew's dilemma, his area of study only deals with *limited non-verbal revelation.*

What questions could we ask? "Is there any evidence that the God of creation wants to have a relationship with us?" We can argue that if God wants to reveal Himself to us, beyond the revelation of His existence, He will find some way of making His desire for a relationship known. If it is at all possible for us to find or discover what it is He wants for us and from us; if we are to know His character and nature, then it is His responsibility as God to not just create us but to reveal Himself, to be knowable.

The scientific mind or the intellectual philosopher of religion places the entire weight of discovering truth about the creator of the universe upon themselves. This might be an exercise in futility! It certainly is an exercise of man's limited ability to discover truth about God. So, the burden of proof, beyond that of God's existence, that He desires a relationship with His created beings, does not fall upon His creation to discover, but upon Him Who Is (God) to make Himself known.

After compiling the limited revelations received by observing the world around us, all future discovery now turns to a literary work that we call "the Bible." We turn our attention away from non-verbal discovery to verbal revelation, to language, culture, and the printed word. Words that are God-breathed. Illumination that is fully dependent upon God speaking directly into the hearts and minds of men.

It is quite a fascinating world, but it is also a dangerous world. Not a treacherous, ominous world, but a world that requires the seeker to walk by faith and not by sight, to trust in the voice of God and not our sole counsel, to humbly approach our receiving of revelation as a gift and not collected as a possession. Revelation that one is called to reverentially share with one's neighbor. We are to understand that no matter how deeply we mine the Scriptures for the truths that they contain, we will never exhaust nor completely attain all the knowledge deposited within.

Here is a fair warning. We must be cautious and disciplined as we begin to interact with these "words" because the words that are used to reveal God are the same words common among the languages of men and we have often mistaken these "words" of men and make God look more like man than the wholly other He really is.

VI

The Godhead:
The Shema and the Trinity

We now begin to focus our attention on what we would call "verbal revelation" of God. We call it "verbal revelation" because the means of transmission or conveyance of this revelation involves the use of language. The book that is most specific to our study is the Bible because it is the exclusively infallible source of revelation about God's nature, character, personhood, and will. In its original hand (original manuscripts) there were only three languages used to record what Paul describes as God-breathed words.

> 2 Timothy 3:16-17 16 "All Scripture is God-breathed and is useful for teaching, rebuking, correcting and training in righteousness, 17 so that the man of God may be thoroughly equipped for every good work."

The Bible was originally written in Hebrew, Aramaic and Greek. We believe and profess that the author of Scripture is God Himself. Yes, He used human instruments to perform the act of writing, but God was their source of inspiration. Since God is the source of inspiration, He is also the guarantor that all subject matter, whether historical, revelational, or inspirational, is also inerrant. And while there are multiple reasons and layers of understanding that we can find within the content of Scripture, we do understand that Scripture itself has a purposed destiny. Meaning what is written within Scripture is destined to be fulfilled.

> John 19:28 [28] "Later, knowing that all was now completed, and *so that the Scripture would be fulfilled, ..."*

The revelation of Scripture is not simply a storehouse of knowledge preserved from antiquated times, it contains content that is alive, it has a living component which contains information of things yet to come. While it recalls divine and human history, it also speaks of things that are now present and profoundly incorporates things that will be.

The scriptures bear witness to things past, present, and future.

Through Verbal Revelation we perceive that there is a culturally Hebraic concept that we might not normally pick up on and therefore be able to consciously reflect upon. Scripture reveals things past, present and future, and Scripture says this of God its author that He is "the same yesterday and today and forever". This is another way of declaring that God is eternal.

> Genesis 21:33   33 "Abraham planted a tamarisk tree in Beersheba, and there he called upon the name of the LORD, the Eternal God."

There is one person in the Bible who makes the claim of being God and Eternal. His name is Jesus.

> Hebrews 13:8   8 "Jesus Christ is the same yesterday and today and forever."

We may not know the author of the book of Hebrews, but we know the author of the book of Revelation. John the Beloved writes an amazing verse of revelation about God confirming that He is eternal.

> Revelation 1:8 ⁸ "I am the Alpha and the Omega," says the Lord God, "who is, and who was, and who is to come, the Almighty."

The "Alpha and Omega" are the first and last letters in the Greek alphabet and both correspond to the "Aleph and the Tav", the first and last letters in the Hebrew Aleph-bet. Interpretively they simply mean "the first and the last" which is a Hebraic way of saying "I am Eternal." Then John gives the name or names of the speaker declaring Him to be the "Lord God". Both are capitalized to denote that they are actual names of God, "Yahweh Elohim". What is a spoken self-description by Yahweh Elohim is this: "who is, who was, and who is to come," or "I am the present, I am the past and I am the future."

What is He saying? He (God) is eternal. But who is "Yahweh Elohim" of whom John declares to be speaking? Why, none other than Jesus.

> Revelation 1:1 "The revelation of Jesus Christ,..."

From these verses our understanding of the Godhead is that there is *one* in the Godhead who is call "Yahweh Elohim" and He is Jesus the Messiah (Christ). But I said "one" in the Godhead. Is there a hint of more than "one"?

Let us continue with John's Revelation in verse 1.

> Revelation 1:1 "The revelation of Jesus Christ, **_which God gave_** him to show his servants what must soon take place."

As God is true to Himself and never changing, He is without beginning and He has no end. The revelations contained within His scriptures carry these same properties meaning they are eternally charged and eternally true. And in this manner, Scripture, which is a revelation of its eternal author is therefore eternal in its purpose and message. There is not a single portion of Scripture that can ever be considered archaic or irrelevant.

> Luke 21:33 ³³ "Heaven and earth will pass away, but my words will never pass away."

In Scripture God defines himself as the one who was, is and is to come; therefore, as we interpret Scripture, especially in our effort to discover and understand God, these revealed discoveries also progress forward demanding their fulfillment.

In reflecting upon John 19:28, what could possibly be meant by the words "that Scripture be fulfilled"? Let us think of it in terms related to an eternal God. If God is eternal, is He ever fully finished? And you can say "well it appears that after creation God rested" so, yes, He was finished creating. If that was God's whole intent, to just create, you might be correct in thinking that His work was finished. But if He gave purpose to what He created, a purpose that would bring glory to His name, and that mankind was created to be in a relationship with God, then creation has a greater purpose than to simply exist. Human beings especially were intended to search out the purpose of their existence.

It is necessary for God to be involved in the discovery process, which means God was not finished creating. Even though we might call it an end, God calls it a beginning. For our eternal God does not exist neither is He bound to a timeline, and while, in our eyes, somethings seemed to be completed, in God's eyes, they are merely 'whole' or 'complete' and are now set in motion toward a fulfillment that is and will eternally be ongoing.

An example of this would come from the cross. Jesus uttered these words "It is finished."

> John 19:30 "When he had received the drink, Jesus said**, "It is finished."** With that, he bowed his head and gave up his spirit."

What was 'finished' was something preordained to be fulfilled; the Lamb of God slain for the salvation of men. This fulfilled plan of God has no end, neither will the work ever be rescinded. This work continually offers eternal security.

> Revelation 13:8 8 "And all that dwell upon the earth shall worship him, whose names are not written in the book of life of the Lamb slain from the foundation of the world."

Yes, His pre-resurrected earthly life came to an end. But what was finished through His earthly life ushered in a continuation of that same eternal work of salvation.

To discover God, we return solely to the Bible as our source of inspiration and truth, where our discovery will eventually lead is to a revelation that God exists in more than one person. In Christianity we have adapted the term Trinity to describe this unique relationship in the Godhead. The word Trinity is not found in the Bible, but it is a wonderful word that helps us to express our belief that there are at least three persons existing in unity in the Godhead.

In an email (November 17, 2020), Rev Lon Wiskell D.Min., writes "The Messianic Jewish Movement prefers to use "the triune nature of God" which is more sustainable in Hebraic thought. While in seminary I learned the 'U.E.D.' of the Godhead - *unity, equality* and *distinctiveness*. Early Christian heresies violated either one or several of these concepts. I would add to the U.E.D. that each member of the Trinity is in *relationship* with each other and in covenant relationship with humanity – 'U.E.D.R.'. I also like Dr. Wess Pinkham's 'perichoresis' – meaning 'the love dance of the Father, the Son and the Spirit' as it represents a dynamic picture of their relationship as they dance together in perfect *harmony*."

The Shema and the Trinity

We will look to provide evidence of this from the Bible, to be found in both current Christian and ancient Judean thought and faith. But before we do that, I would like to clear up any misconceptions of the Godhead that is proffered by modern Judaism. For modern Judaism rejects the idea of the Trinity and it is done so primarily on the basis of one passage of Scripture. This portion of Scripture is called the "shema." That passage is Deuteronomy 6:4.

> Deuteronomy 6:4 "Hear, O Israel: The LORD our God, the LORD is one."

Or in the Hebrew: "Shema Israel, Yahweh Elohenu Yahweh Echad". (Read from right to left.)

שְׁמַע יִשְׂרָאֵל יְהוָה אֱלֹהֵינוּ יְהוָה אֶחָד׃

NOTE: "Shema" means "listen" or "hear."

Rabbi Neil Gillman writes: "by any measure, the one passage in all of Scripture that every Jew, no matter what his or her identification with Judaism, will recognize is Deuteronomy 6:4, commonly known as "the Shema." It appears more frequently in our traditional (*Judaic*) liturgy than any other single passage in the Bible. Worshiping Jews recite it daily, morning and evening, and more frequently on the Sabbath and festivals. It is also* the most ancient biblical passage to be incorporated into our liturgy, dating at least from the days of the Second Temple (400 BC to 70 AD). It has been the traditional "last word" of Jewish martyrs throughout the ages, and to this day pious Jews pray that they may be able to recite this verse as death approaches.

NOTE: "'the Shema' is the watchword for the Jewish faith" Dr. Barri Cae Seif. 10/28/2020.

In its original context, the verse is part of Moses' extended sermon to the Israelites prior to his death and to their entering the Promise Land. Moses begins by exhorting the people to revere God and to observe and obey God's Torah so that they may increase and prosper in the land that God has promised to them. Then comes the 'Shema', followed immediately by an exhortation familiar to Christians, "love the Lord your God with all your heart with all your soul and with all your might." [17.]

> Matthew 22:37 37 "Jesus replied: "'Love the Lord your God with all your heart and with all your soul and with all your mind.'"

Gillman continues. "But the Shema verse has suffered the fate of other familiar texts: it has come to be recited almost mindlessly, with little attention to what it really means. ...in fact, its meaning is not all that obvious." [18.]

The final word in the Shema is the Hebrew word 'echad' and within modern Judaism is almost exclusively understood to mean a numerical number one. "...It is not at all clear what it means to claim that any single being is in fact "one." [19.] (*The intended*) meaning is that God is singular in His being. It is also used to express the exclusivity of God." [20.]

To many Jews, they hold that the Christian notion of the Trinity dilutes Judaism's strong monotheistic components. But this depends on how we interpret "the Lord is one" since echad also means 'one in unity'. Buried deep within the interpretive memory of Judaism's long past is a rendering more closely affiliated with

Christianity's understanding of "the Lord is one".

Maimonides was a Sephardic Jewish sage and philosopher who lived in Egypt during the Middle Ages (1138 - 1204) and left Judaism with a set of Thirteen Principles of Faith. He did not neglect to write his thoughts on the 'shema' regarding what "the Lord is one" means. To Maimonides, the mystery of God and His true being is known internally to God Himself. In other words, God is not a mystery to Himself. He has full knowledge of who and what He is.

What does this mean to Christians? Maimonides would use this understanding to exclude the possibility of God existing in three persons. But we see from this understanding that God, intricately and intrinsically knows Himself, even while existing as three persons in one being. God fully knows Himself, what He thinks, what He will do, and how He will do it without contradicting Himself. For us, if we existed as three persons, each person would have very little knowledge of what they truly think and how they would truly behave. God as Trinity, always acts in unity because "the Lord is one."

This attribute, "the Lord being one", is surrounded in the mystery of God's knowledge. "For God's knowledge is intrinsic to God's nature. God is intrinsically knowledge, and God's essence is knowledge itself. This leads to the claim that God is simultaneously the subject of knowledge (the One who knows), the verb or activity of knowing, [the One who acts or principal cause] and the object of knowledge (that which is known). ...To claim that God is "one" is to insist that God is not only syntactically but also metaphysically [the] subject, verb, and object-- all at the same time, all eternally and without change. To put it another way, God is "knowledge knowing knowledge," or "knowledge knowing itself." For Maimonides, that's what "the shema" means when it affirms that God is "one." [21]

What takeaway meaning does this offer the believer in Messiah? It brings us a little closer to the understanding of the mystery of God's existence in Trinity. As we go forward, as we search out Scriptures that speak of Father, Son and Holy Spirit, they will help us to capture the personhood of God. But His essence and divine nature cannot be fully understood within these titles alone. Within God's very being, He is so completely one and fully in control of His unchanging nature that He internally cannot, nor will He ever, be conflicted over anything He engages in.

As the Father, or the Son, or the Holy Spirit, His infinitely discerning knowledge of Himself makes all that He is "one." As was described above, God is both the subject, verb, and object of His self-existing Spirit. One thing we can declare is that "God is one" is about the eternal integrity of God's very being.

VII

The Godhead: Father

Psalm 68:3-5   ³ 'But may the righteous be glad and rejoice before God; may they be happy and joyful. ⁴ Sing to God, sing praise to his name, extol him who rides on the clouds--his name is the LORD-- and rejoice before him. ⁵ A father to the fatherless, a defender of widows, is God in his holy dwelling.'

Psalm 89:26   ²⁶ "He will call out to me, 'You are my Father, my God, the Rock my Savior.''

Isaiah 9:6 ⁶ "For to us a child is born, to us a son is given, and the government will be on his shoulders. And he will be called Wonderful Counselor, Mighty God, Everlasting Father, Prince of Peace."

Malachi 2:10   ¹⁰ "Have we not all one Father? Did not one God create us? Why

> do we profane the covenant of our fathers by breaking faith with one another?"

Through the study of Scripture, we begin to focus our attention upon the multiple revelations of God through His many names, terms and actions. Most of these are anthropomorphic (literally: human and body like) since the names and terms that describe mankind are taken and applied to the character, nature and actions of an unseen supernatural God who is spirit. Zoomorphic is a term for describing God in terms using animal characteristics - like wings of an eagle or of a mother hen. This is a very Hebraic concept and expression that many people do not understand.

By the inspiration of His Spirit, God uses the language of men to reveal himself. As God describes himself in human terms, such as father or son, these human images of God are always somewhat incomplete. Why is that? It is because God in essence is *totally other* than who we are, thereby rendering our comprehension of Him quite less than complete.

It would be wrong to say that this form of revelation is inadequate as that would be an indictment against God's ability or willingness to make Himself known. But we might think so only if we feel God must answer all of the questions we ask about Him to our satisfaction. In doing so we are saying to God that He needs to change the parameters of the purposes behind what He has chosen to reveal about Himself to us. I believe I would rather let God decide what I need to know about Him because I suspect His revelation to be much more important. I would also go so far as to believe that even what God chose to omit was irrelevant to the overall message of Scripture.

From the selected Scriptures that we have cited above we see that God is being called or described as father. What can we know of God as father from just these scriptures? As father He is the LORD God, Israel's eternal father, rock of our salvation, the one who created us, father to the fatherless and judge (in this context God is the one who executes justice) to the widows, the father of everyone, He is holy.

God as Father is the one who originates the being and purpose for man and the universe. Because of this, Israel and the writers of Scripture recognize man's dependence upon God. Why? Because God never intended man to do anything without including Him. We could think of the sinful disobedience on the part of Adam and Eve as an attempt by them to seek independence from God, something we call the "I will" syndrome.

The Old Testament, describing God as "father", carried a two-part revelation of the function of the first person in the Godhead. The first was that God as Father is the one who was the giver of life and He instilled within this gift of life purpose. The second is that he is also the inspirational visionary who leads us towards the fulfillment of life's purpose. So, when we speak of the first person in the Godhead, we are in effect saying that He is the Father; our visionary leader who has ordained purpose for an inspired life.

This revelation of God as father only distinguishes the work of the first person in the triune Godhead. The other terms that we will deal with are the Son and Holy Spirit, names given to the second and third person in the Godhead. It must be clearly understood that they exist in complete union with one another and in total agreement to what has been given life and the inspirational purpose that this created life has been given.

As the father, who is the giver of life and the inspiration for that life, God has purposed to put Himself into His creation thereby looking for that created life to be a reflection of Himself. This reality is built into our human existence that as human fathers beget offspring, others will look upon the offspring and see the resemblance of the father.

Recognizing this is not an admission that we put ourselves and our humanity back upon God, but the reality is that God continues to place Himself and who He is and what His will is for our lives, upon us His creation. The transference of revelation concerning Himself and His will for mankind onto His creation is not blasphemous but harmonious. God is a God of order, purpose, unity and patterns, and His creation is to be a reflection of that same order, purpose, unity and patterns.

So, even in the revelation of God as Father we see types within the Scriptures that help us to gain a greater understanding of these things. These things that are order, purpose, unity and patterns.

One of these types is found in the book of Genesis Chapter 22. The story is about the binding of Isaac or in Hebrew it is called the "Akedah". It takes 18 verses to tell the entire story, but I want to focus on four of them.

> Genesis 22:1-2 [1] "Sometime later God tested Abraham. He said to him, "Abraham!" "Here I am," he replied. [2] Then God said, "Take your son, your only son, Isaac, whom you love, and go to the region of Moriah. Sacrifice him there as a burnt offering on one of the mountains I will tell you about."

> Genesis 22:11-12 ^{11} "But the angel of the LORD called out to him from heaven, "Abraham! Abraham!" "Here I am," he replied. ^{12} "Do not lay a hand on the boy," he said. "Do not do anything to him. Now I know that you fear God, because you have not withheld from me your son, your only son."

This story has been challenging for many who recognize that the commandment given to Abraham was totally out of character of a loving and just God. But what was equally uncharacteristic is that Abraham seemed uncompromising and very willing to obey such a foreign command. Isaac is Abraham's son. But he is more than just a son, he is the son of prophetic promise. He would be a part of a long line of Abraham's offspring who would bring blessing to the nations.

Strangely Isaac, whom various Jewish sages believed was of a mature age, perhaps thirty years old at this time, without resisting, gave himself over to his father's will. Together they built the altar and placed kindling on the altar.

Then Isaac allowed his father to bind him and place him on the altar as the sacrifice. Within moments of Abraham raising his knife to kill his son the Lord intervenes and offers a substitute sacrifice in place of Isaac.

Specific words had been exchanged regarding Isaac as "your son, your only son," that helps us to begin to understand the purpose for such a request by God to Abraham. For in this particular role, Abraham is attested as a 'father' and Isaac is clearly a 'son'. Abraham's obedience proved his devotion to God, more specifically the inspirational will of God. God steps in and provides an alternate sacrifice. God steps into the role of father and the alternate sacrifice takes on the role of the son. We move forward through the passages of Scripture and time to come to a story where God the Father willingly offers up His "only Son" to be the sacrifice, our alternate sacrifice, for the sins of the world.

One might imagine that this kind of spiritual interpretation and understanding could only be ascertained following the remarkable death, burial and resurrection of Jesus. That a deep understanding of the function of God as Father could only be fully developed after the resurrection. But I believe that is a wrong assumption.

In modern Judaism during morning and evening prayers, during specific or special days of worship that incorporate written prayers and liturgies, we find many references to their "Father in Heaven". For most of these are not modern in their creation but have been rediscovered to go back through the ages to a time even before that of Jesus the Messiah. "During Rosh Hashanah the Jewish people stand before God and celebrate the creation and continued existence of the world. Again and again, they will address their Creator as *Avinu Malkeinu* (Our Father, Our King). [22.]

Their interpretive understanding of God as Father is ancient. But how ancient? Well, at least back to the time of Abraham and I would not be surprised to find evidence of such a position of understanding even earlier.

To the Jewish people Abraham is seen as their father, both as a natural father and as a spiritual father and that understanding is carried over into the New Testament.

> John 8:56 "Your father Abraham rejoiced at the thought of seeing my day; he saw it and was glad."

This passage just doesn't confirm the regard the children of Israel had towards Abraham; it goes beyond that. Something was given to Abraham through his encounters with God that not only revealed God to be his Father but that those encounters were prophetic revelations of God's Messiah. Not only do we interpret the binding of Isaac as a revelation about God the Father who willingly offered His Son as a sacrifice, but apparently so did Abraham. "Abraham rejoiced at the thought of seeing my day; he saw it and was glad."

It is supernaturally discerned. Abraham took the revelations given to him and allowed his God to broaden his understanding. Paul writes of this.

> Romans 4:16 "Therefore, the promise comes by faith, so that it may be by grace and may be guaranteed to all Abraham's offspring-- not only to those who are of the law but also to those who are of the faith of Abraham. He is the father of us all."

Abraham was not only a natural father but a spiritual father as well who lived by faith and was granted spiritual eyes to see what his Spiritual Father was orchestrating through His Son, Messiah.

> Hebrews 11:17-19 [17] "By faith Abraham, when God tested him, offered Isaac as a sacrifice. He who had received the promises was about to sacrifice his one and only son, [18] even though God had said to him, "It is through Isaac that your offspring will be reckoned." [19] Abraham reasoned that God could raise the dead, and figuratively speaking, he did receive Isaac back from death."

James 2:21-23 ²¹ "Was not our ancestor Abraham considered righteous for what he did when he offered his son Isaac on the altar? ²² You see that his faith and his actions were working together, and his faith was made complete by what he did. ²³ And the scripture was fulfilled that says, "Abraham believed God, and it was credited to him as righteousness," and he was called God's friend."

The 1ˢᵗ person in the Godhead is the Father!

Isaiah 63:16 ¹⁶ "But you are our Father, though Abraham does not know us or Israel acknowledge us; you, O LORD, are our Father, our Redeemer from of old is your name."

VIII

The Godhead: Son – Jesus

Psalm 2:1-12 ¹ "Why do the nations conspire and the peoples plot in vain? ² The kings of the earth take their stand and the rulers gather together against the LORD and against his Anointed One. ³ "Let us break their chains," they say, "and throw off their fetters." ⁴ The One enthroned in heaven laughs; the Lord scoffs at them. ⁵ Then he rebukes them in his anger and terrifies them in his wrath, saying, ⁶ "I have installed my King on Zion, my holy hill." ⁷ I will proclaim the decree of the LORD: He said to me, "You are my Son; today I have become your Father. ⁸ Ask of me, and I will make the nations your inheritance, the ends of the earth your possession. ⁹ You will rule them with an iron scepter; you will dash them to pieces like pottery." ¹⁰ Therefore, you kings, be wise; be warned, you rulers of the earth. ¹¹ Serve the LORD with fear and rejoice

> with trembling. ¹² Kiss the Son, lest he be angry and you be destroyed in your way, for his wrath can flare up in a moment. Blessed are all who take refuge in him."

These next Sacred Journey chapters will be the most spiritually stirring chapters for me to write. These chapters will speak of the second person of the Godhead. It is the second person of the Godhead who will be the revelation of the Father to men.

> John 5:37 ³⁷ "And the Father who sent me has himself testified concerning me. You have never heard his voice nor seen his form,"

> John 6:46 ⁴⁶ "No one has seen the Father except the one who is from God; only he has seen the Father."

It is the second person of the Godhead whose purpose it is to complete the will of the Father.

> John 5:43 ⁴³ "I have come in my Father's name,..."

This second person of the Godhead will bear the image of the Father.

> John 14:9-11 ⁹ "Jesus answered: "Don't you know me, Philip, even after I have

been among you such a long time? Anyone who has seen me has seen the Father. How can you say, 'Show us the Father'? [10] Don't you believe that I am in the Father, and that the Father is in me? The words I say to you are not just my own. Rather, it is the Father, living in me, who is doing his work. [11] Believe me when I say that I am in the Father and the Father is in me;"

The second person of the Godhead will be the one with whom mankind will interact, form a relationship, be given direction for their behavior, and He will be their redeemer.

1 John 1:2-3 [2] "The life appeared; we have seen it and testify to it, and we proclaim to you the eternal life, which was with the Father and has appeared to us. [3] We proclaim to you what we have seen and heard, so that you also may have fellowship with us. And our fellowship is with the Father and with his Son, Jesus Christ."

John 8:38 [38] "I am telling you what I have seen in the Father's presence,"

> John 14:12-13 ¹² "I tell you the truth, anyone who has faith in me will do what I have been doing. He will do even greater things than these, because I am going to the Father. ¹³ And I will do whatever you ask in my name, so that the Son may bring glory to the Father."

I will not hide the fact that I believe that the second person in the Godhead is none other than Jesus of Nazareth for Jesus of Nazareth made the same claim.

We will examine a lot of those claims in the coming chapters but right now it is my intent to first search out some Jewish and Christian Old Testament revelations of the second person in the Godhead. Modern Judaism is not necessarily hiding historical positions that she once held in the past concerning the Godhead, but she is not necessarily forthcoming or even feeling at all compelled to share everything it once interpretively believed on this matter.

Fortunately, there are some Jewish scholars who are willing to share and confess certain positions of faith that they once held to be true. One of our goals is to discover what they once believed concerning a second person in the Godhead. Another is to move from here into a deep revelation of that same person from both the Old and the New Testaments.

Where to begin? Perhaps a couple of clarifying statements are in order. First, I believe it is necessary to understand that current and historical writings reveal that the Jewish people, both ancient and modern, were never completely in agreement about what they believed concerning the revelation of God in Scripture. Even while strong attempts have been made to form one unified set of doctrines and practices through the study of the same Hebrew Scriptures and other theological writings, it has never happened, for the ancient Judeans, modern Judaism or Christianity.

If we would just look at the time of Messiah's first coming we would discover, as of the time of this writing, over thirty-two sects are recognized to have existed. What does this mean? It means they held differing views on various issues of belief and practice. Note that these differences didn't necessarily lead to conflict and separation. In most cases they did not. In some cases, while still united by central tenets of their faith, these varying views could and would create isolated communities who withdrew from the mainstream body of Jews to worship as they believed it proper for them. These sects were of course minorities.

The majority of ancient biblical Jews (Judeans) were united behind a commonly held set of beliefs and practices. The belief that there was a second person in the Godhead is considered to be that of the majority. What this means is that modern Judaism has moved away from this particular belief, a belief they once held, and Christianity has forgotten this fact.

Dr. Daniel Boyarin writes: "once the temple was destroyed in A.D. 70, ... Some Jews wished to continue sacrifices as best they could, while others rejected such practices entirely. Some Jews thought that the purity practices that were important in Temple times were still to be practiced, while others thought they were irrelevant.

There were, moreover, different interpretations of the Torah, different sets of ideas about God, different notions of how to practice the law. In Jerusalem, which had been re-founded by priests and teachers [having] returned from the Babylonian exile (538 BC), new religious ideas and practices had been developed, many of them adopted by a group called the Pharisees, who, apparently, were rather aggressively promoting these ideas among the Jews living outside of Jerusalem who had different traditions and practices, the so-called people of the land, those who had not gone into exile in Babylonia." [23.]

Are there other interesting things that can be said about the diversity within their beliefs?
Boyarin continues: "So being religiously Jewish [back] then was a much more complicated affair than it is even now. There were no rabbis yet, and even the priests in Jerusalem and around the countryside were divided among themselves. Not only that, but

there were many Jews both in Palestine and outside of it, in places such as Alexandria in Egypt, who had very different ideas about what being a good, devout Jew meant. Some believed that in order to be a kosher Jew you had to believe in a single divine figure and any other belief was simply idol worship.

Others believed that God had a divine deputy or emissary or even son, exalted above all the angels, who functioned as an intermediary between God and the world in creation, revelation and redemption. Many Jews believed that redemption was going to be effected by a human being, an actual hidden scion [i.e. offspring] of the house of David-- an Anastasia [i.e. resurrected one]-- who at a certain point would take up the scepter and the sword, defeat Israel's enemies, and return her to her former glory.

Others believed that the redemption was going to be affected [caused] by that same second divine figure mentioned above and not a human being at all. And still others believed that these two were one and the same, that the

Messiah of David would be the divine Redeemer." **24.**

What could cause the disparity that created such divergent and opposing views? Basically, it comes down to a difference in interpretive methods as well as the need for commanding an overall comprehension of Scriptural revelation. I believe that this last part might be the most challenging. We might think that the concept of a second person in the Godhead, one that we would describe as knowable, would not be too difficult to uncover. In fact, from a Gentile Christian perspective we might think that most of the hard evidence is located in the New Testament.

We might even say that there is a lack of sufficient evidence in the Old Testament for this particular understanding of the Godhead. This last understanding might help to explain why modern Judaism currently seems to reject a conclusion that there is a Father and Son in the Godhead. Why modern Rabbinic Judaism seems to basically reject the idea of a triune

God has very little to do with their historic interpretive understanding of the subject.

I would say that the reason for such views, on two or more persons in the Godhead has more to do with the "over-abundance" of biblical revelation than the lack thereof. It is quite possible that it is the multiplicity of revelations concerning the second person in the Godhead that can leave the best of scholars pleasantly excited while still perplexed.

The challenge is to be able to put together a comprehensive and systematic catalog of every reference, name, action and attribute of this second person. The complexity of such a challenge should not be regarded as being overwhelming but is instead awe inspiring. That is why my query earlier was 'where do I begin?'

Perhaps the place to start is not to attempt to list all of the innumerable references and revelations of the second person in the Godhead, but to make an attempt to explain why I believe there are so many. The explanation begins with Genesis 1 verse three.

> Genesis 1:3 "And God said, "Let there be light," and there was light."

וַיֹּאמֶר אֱלֹהִים יְהִי אוֹר וַיְהִי־ אוֹר:

(read from right to left)

Here is a literal translation of the Hebrew text. "And said Elohim "He becomes light, and he is becoming light."

This is God speaking quite profoundly to Himself about Himself. In Genesis 1:1 we are told that God created everything. In verse 3 on day one of creation, God speaks. This is the method God uses each of the first six days that He was creating. The ancient sages determined that what was created on day one did not seem to conform to the same parameters as those things created over the next five days. As they carefully considered <u>its</u> uniqueness was somehow other, outside or above the rest of creation. The sages concluded that, though being separated from creation, <u>it</u> was meant *for* creation. It became a mystery waiting to be uncovered.

God appeared to them to be speaking to Himself and calling Himself 'light'. Did this mean He was transforming Himself? No, that would mean God can change and we have already concluded in earlier study that God does not change. [25.] It meant that God would be a "light" to His creation. Meaning, He would become that Divine necessity which all of creation would need to live. He would be revelation, truth, and illumination. One may ask how much revelation, truth and illumination does creation need to live? Apparently an unlimited amount.

A few millennia later King David would write:

> Psalm 36:9 "For with you is the fountain of life; in your light we see light."

Let me repeat, *"in your light we see light."*

Hebraic logic runs like this:

I. Light and Wisdom are joined because they both bring Life
II. The owner of Life is also the author of Wisdom
III. God is the owner of Life
IV. Light reveals Life and Wisdom
V. God is therefore Light
VI. The Second Person (Son) is Light
VII. The Second Person (Son) is God

In Genesis 1:3 the 2nd Person in the Godhead is speaking over Himself. He would be the 'light,' the revelation of Himself, to His creation. This revelation is going to require a whole lot of words!

> John 3:19 "This is the verdict: Light has come into the world, but men loved darkness instead of light because their deeds were evil."

> John 8:12 "When Jesus spoke again to the people, he said, "I am the light of the world. Whoever follows me will never

walk in darkness, but will have the light of life."

John 12:46 "I have come into the world as a light, so that no one who believes in me should stay in darkness."

The second person in the Godhead is the Son!

IX

The Godhead:
Son – Messiah

In the last chapter I stated plainly that I believe the second person in the Godhead is none other than Jesus of Nazareth, meaning that I believe he was God who also took on the flesh of his creation. Being God, the second person of the Godhead made himself known to his creation, especially his people Israel, through various manifestations and forms. But when he would come in the flesh, when he would be God incarnate, he would take upon himself a predetermined mantle of service. That particular mantle, that servant, was given the title Messiah.

Messiah, Son of David, and Messiah Son of Joseph

I would like to take this opportunity to deal with two of the expectant revelations found within Scripture that would give us a foundation for what we are to believe about Messiah the 2nd Person in the Godhead.

Christianity accepts two predominant claims concerning the incarnate scope and ministry of God's Jewish Messiah. It is not my intention to examine all messianic prophecies, but for the moment I would like to look at two of the main claims of messianic expectation. These two claims are popularly known as Messiah, Son of David, the reigning King, and Messiah Son of Joseph, the Suffering Servant.

What is the origin of these claims?
"MESSIAH: Originally referring primarily to someone anointed by Yahweh into a specific role as a prophet, priest or especially King, the term *messiah* is also applied more widely to cover a hoped-for redeemer figure who emerges in the Old Testament-- a figure that Christians affirm is fulfilled in Jesus. Intertestamental texts (e.g., *T.Sim.* 7:1-2) seem to expect a priestly savior as well as a royal one, while the Qumran community may have anticipated a prophetic messiah too. (1QS IX, 9-11; 1Q28a II, 11-21 [cf Jn 1:91-28]).[26]
Christianity accepts all of these claims, redeeming figure, priestly savior, royal one and prophetic messiah.

The term "anointed one" translates the Hebrew "*Mashiach*". [27.] The Greek equivalent is "*Christos*", or Christ.

"The belief in the Messiah son of David and the Messiah son of Joseph already existed in the time of Judas Maccabeus (200 BC -130 BC), in whose time the 'Vision of the Seventy Shepherds' in the Book of Enoch was written." [28.]

At one time, "the rabbinic theory of two Messiahs, the Messiah son of Joseph and the Messiah son of David, was widespread during the Second Temple Period (450 BC - 70 AD)." [29.]

While the development of this theory continued post the Second Temple Period, nevertheless, it demonstrates that these viewpoints, concerning two Messiahs, ran deep in the Jewish consciousness from ancient to modern times.

Christianity has always embraced both of these messianic claims as they had been in the interpretative understanding of Messiah prior to the appearance of Jesus of Nazareth. The Son of David claim originates with the covenant God made with David recorded in 2nd Samuel 7:1-17. "Of particular importance was that David's dynasty would hold the kingdom in perpetuity (2 Samuel 7:13) so that his throne would forever be secure (verse 16)". [30]

> 2 Samuel 7:13,16 [13] "He is the one who will build a house for my Name, and I will establish the throne of his kingdom forever... [16] Your house and your kingdom will endure forever before me; your throne will be established forever."

"The exile {of the 10 northern tribes of Israel} to Assyria in the 7th century B.C. triggered reflection on how this promise could be fulfilled in the absence of a Davidic monarchy, but rather than rejecting the Davidic hope, this promise was then expressed in specifically eschatological terms. (e.g., Ezekiel 37:24-28)" [31]

Ezekiel 37:24-28 24 "My servant David will be king over them, and they will all have one shepherd. They will follow my laws and be careful to keep my decrees. 25 They will live in the land I gave to my servant Jacob, the land where your fathers lived. They and their children and their children's children will live there forever, and David my servant will be their prince forever. 26 I will make a covenant of peace with them; it will be an everlasting covenant. I will establish them and increase their numbers, and I will put my sanctuary among them forever. 27 My dwelling place will be with them; I will be their God, and they will be my people. 28 Then the nations will know that I the LORD make Israel holy, when my sanctuary is among them forever."

The door was open for further messianic interpretive expectations in the form of other fulfillments. Zechariah 12:10 is a good example:

¹⁰ "And I will pour out on the house of David and the inhabitants of Jerusalem a spirit of grace and supplication. They will look on me, the one they have pierced, and they will mourn for him as one mourns for an only child, and grieve bitterly for him as one grieves for a firstborn son."

Messiah, son of Joseph

The ancient Judean sages also applied this passage "to the tragic end of Messiah Son of Joseph: he is the one, who at the End of Days, will be pierced and killed by the wicked and Gentile forces." [32.]

"At first, the Messiah son of Joseph was not a tragic figure: he was to be the eschatological commander and chief of the armed forces of Israel. The motif of his tragic end is attested with certainty in rabbinic sources not earlier than the second half of the third century A.D., and the event is almost always based upon Zechariah 12:10: the man 'whom they have pierced' was identified with Messiah son of Joseph." [33]

Messiah, son of David

Messiah, identified as the son of David, provides an accepted claim found within both Christianity and Rabbinical Judaism and in reality "Christians, like Jews are still waiting to see their interpretations borne out by [future] events." [34]

Messiah son of David would establish the kingdom without end and would usher in an age of peace, prosperity and justice "by defeating all agents of oppression, both human and superhuman." [35]

This Messiah's coming would be "in clouds of glory (heaven)... (Daniel 7:13)." [36]

> Daniel 7:13 "In my vision at night I looked, and there before me was one like a son of man, coming with the clouds of heaven. He approached the Ancient of Days and was led into his presence."

Rabbinic Judaism has rejected the man Jesus of Nazareth as being the Messiah. The assertion is that he did not fulfill this specific prophetic claim, and of course they were right. But this doesn't disqualify Jesus from being the Judean/Jewish Messiah. Even though current Rabbinic Judaism teaches that they are to only expect one coming of Messiah, (the Messiah son of David), ***that was not the position of the ancient Judeans*** during the time prior to and during the earthly ministry of Jesus.

The Two Comings of Messiah

The interpretive understanding and faith of the Judeans included a second claim on the servant ministry of Messiah which would point to two separate comings.

"Initially the only difference between "Christians" and "Jews" was that the former [Christians] believed that the Messiah had already come, while the latter [Jews] believed that he was yet to come." **37.**

Today, some within rabbinical Judaism hold a position that the "idea of messianic suffering, death, and resurrection" came about as an apology after the fact of Jesus' death. "Allegedly, after his death, his followers discovered that Isaiah 53 may be reinterpreted, not as referring to the persecuted people of Israel, but to the suffering Messiah." [38].

Professor Daniel Boyarin responds to such a claim: "... this commonplace view has to be rejected completely. The notion of the humiliated and suffering Messiah was not at all alien within Judaism before Jesus' advent, and it remained current among Jews well into the future following that-- indeed, well into the early modern period. The fascinating (and to some, no doubt, uncomfortable) fact is that this tradition was well documented by modern Messianic Jews, who concerned to demonstrate that their belief in Jesus does not make them un-Jewish. Whether or not one accepts their theology, it remains the case that they have a strong textual base for the view that the suffering servant Messiah is deeply rooted in Jewish texts early and late. Jews

[Judeans] it seems had no difficulty whatever with understanding a Messiah who would vicariously suffer to redeem the world. Once again, what has been allegedly ascribed to Jesus after the fact is, in fact, a piece of entrenched messianic speculation and expectation that was current before Jesus came into the world at all [2nd Temple Period]. That the Messiah would suffer and be humiliated was something Jews learned from close reading of the biblical texts, a close reading in precisely the style of classically rabbinic interpretation that has become known as midrash [message]." [39]

What we can understand from Dr. Boyarin is that from the middle ages, to the more modern and influential Jewish elders/rabbis, while knowing better, willfully discarded their once held messianic expectation of "the suffering servant or son of Joseph" on purpose. "Even though these same Jewish Scholars understood from Scripture that a Messiah son of Joseph would be slain and resurrected, they refused to continue to recognize and publish such conclusions." [40]

What we need to understand concerning Messiah son of David and Messiah son of Joseph is that even though these claims are no longer mutually held by Christianity and Rabbinic Judaism, they were held by the majority of Judeans/Jews who lived prior to and during the time of Jesus' coming. No one is ever forced to believe what they do not want to believe, but the truth is that the Judeans, living in the late centuries B.C., with a sense of expectancy were looking for the coming of the Messiah Son of David and the Messiah Son of Joseph.

X

The Godhead:
Messiah:
Son of God and Son of Man

We continue our discovery of the second person in the Godhead by exploring some of the most widely accepted titles as being connected to Messiah. And each title that we discover being applied to Messiah carries with it revelation of the nature, character of Messiah and His heavenly and earthly ministry. The first revelation we dealt with, of the second person in the Godhead, was that of "Son". That title helped us to differentiate the second person in the Godhead from the first person in the Godhead whom we called "Father". These terms are applied to their supernatural spiritual existence. In the last chapter we dealt with the titles Messiah Son of David and Messiah Son of Joseph. These titles are referring to the earthly ministry of the "Son" for they point to Messiah's connection to two earthly ancestors, Joseph and David.

There are two other titles that speak of Messiah being "Son" and are quite illuminating because they joined the two ideas together. The first idea presented the Son as being the second person in the Godhead and the second as being a son of mankind. Just as Messiah Son of David and Messiah Son of Joseph are names for Jesus, the other titles, Son of God and Son of Man, are also applied to Jesus.

Son of God and Son of Man are two titles found within the New Testament. Their interpretive meanings, with regard to the biblical messianic understanding (Messiah Jesus in particular), have been the subject of much discussion (and mild debate) by biblical scholars for many centuries without resulting in a definitive resolution for those of the Christian faith or Rabbinical Judaism.

As we interpretively unwrap these messianic titles let us ask this question first. "What are the meanings of these two titles in relationship to Jesus?

"Who was Jesus? The conventional view, of course, is that "Son of God" is the decisive title for Jesus. It is by this title that [the man] Jesus is held to be part of the Trinity: Father, Son and Holy Spirit. It is as the "Son of God" that he is worshiped as divine; it is as the Son of God that he was deemed to have been given to be sacrificed in order that the world might be redeemed." [41]

From this do we have a clear understanding of how the title "Son of God" applies to Jesus? "First of all, interestingly enough, the term "son of God" is not often used in referring to Jesus in the New Testament. In the writings of Paul, the most common term [for Jesus] is 'Lord'. In the Gospels, Jesus is more likely to be referred to (or actually to refer to himself) by the title "Son of Man." Most Christians today, if they have thought about it at all, would think that by this title, Son of Man, Jesus' human nature is being designated, while the title "Son of God" refers to his divine nature. This was indeed the interpretation of most of the Fathers of the Church. A new Bible translation called the Common English Bible has gone so far as to translate 'Son of Man' as "the human one"." [42]

Daniel Boyarin continues: "I will show that almost the opposite was the case in the Gospel of Mark: "Son of God" referred to the king of Israel, the earthly king of David's seat, while "Son of Man" referred to a heavenly figure and not a human being at all. The title "Son of Man" denoted Jesus as a part of God, while the title "Son of God" indicated his status as King Messiah. But what is the Messiah, and how does it relate to the Christ? Truth be told, they were exactly the same thing or at any rate the same word." [43]

"The identity of Jesus of Nazareth was central to the early church's self-understanding and its appropriation of its Jewish heritage. The language, imagery, literary forms, and theological conceptions, through which the church expressed itself and its views of reality, were traditional-- a heritage from its culture and environment. The uniqueness of the early church lay in the church's appropriation of this heritage to the figure of Jesus, whom it perceived to be the unique agent of God's activity, and in the modifications of that heritage that resulted from this process of appropriation.

Exegetical and theological exposition of the figure of Jesus, over the centuries has focused on the title *christos* or its Hebrew counterpart *mashiach*, and thus we continue to speak of Christology [the study of the person and literature of the Christ] and of Jesus as 'the Christ.' The nomenclature [system of naming based upon activity] is understandable, given the New Testament's frequent use of "Christ" as a surname for Jesus, which is, in turn, a reflection of their early practice in the church. This early tendency to speak of "Jesus Christ" notwithstanding, the New Testament applies a wide range of titles and terminology to Jesus, and many modern treatises on New Testament Christology are organized according to "Christological titles": Son of God, Son of Man, Lord, Messiah (or Christ), prophet, and the like. The method and terminology are problematic, however.

First, the expression "Christological titles" attaches undue weight to a single title among the many that the early church ascribed to Jesus as it sought to identify him with the various divine agents in Jewish belief and expectation.

Second, categorization according to titles ignores the fact that different titles may attribute the same function or roles to Jesus, and a single title may have a variety of meanings or nuances.

We need an approach to the subject that better suits the data. "Narrative Christology" is an innovative approach that.... The method rightly recognizes that Jesus is a character in a story with a plot that began in the past and continues on into the future. Who or what Jesus was, or is, or will be becomes evident as the plot unfolds and his roles develop." [44].

'Mashiach or Messiah' was a term used in connection with Israel's kings as they were anointed with oil at the time of their ascension to the throne.

"The king is therefore referred to in the Hebrew Bible as the Anointed of YHWH (GOD) or the Mashiach of YHWH. Other Israelite kings who are described as having been anointed with oil on their ascension to the kingship include David (1 Samuel16:3), Solomon (1 Kings 1:34), Jehu (1 Kings 19:16), Joash (2 Kings 11:12), and Jehoahaz (2 Kings 23:30). ...The anointed, earthly king of Israel is adopted by GOD as his son; the 'son of God' is thus the reigning, living king of Israel." [45.]

"Psalms 2 and 110 have supporting verses of this usage...

> Psalm 2:2, 6-7 [2] "The kings of the earth take their stand and the rulers gather together against the LORD and against his Anointed One... [6] "I have installed my King on Zion, my holy hill." [7] I will proclaim the decree of the LORD: He said to me, "You are my Son; today I have become your Father."
>
> Psalm 110:1-2 "The LORD says to my Lord: "Sit at my right hand until I make your enemies a footstool for your feet." [2] The LORD will extend your mighty scepter from Zion; you will rule in the midst of your enemies."

and contribute to the notion of the exalted Christ seated at the right hand of power in Mark 14:62." [46.]

[62] "I am," said Jesus. "And you will see the Son of Man sitting at the right hand of the Mighty One and coming on the clouds of heaven."

"When Mark, in the very beginning of his Gospel writes,

> Mark 1:1 "The beginning of the gospel about Jesus Christ, the Son of God."

the Son of God means the human Messiah, using the old title for the King of the House of David." [47].

"Following the exile and the return of a remnant of Jews to Jerusalem the kingdom of David was without a king. The people prayed for a new king to rule over the house of David, and the seed of this "notion of a promised Redeemer, a new King David whom God would send at the end of days", became part of their Messianic expectations during the Second Temple Period. The term "Son of God" was indeed a messianic title, but one given to "the 'human' Messiah"." [48].

"When, on the other hand, Mark refers to him in the second chapter of his Gospel as the "Son of Man," he is pointing to the divine nature of the Christ. This seems like a paradox: the name of *God* being used for Jesus' human nature, [and] the name 'Man" for his divine nature." **49.**

> Mark 2:10,28 [10] "But that you may know that the Son of Man has authority on earth to forgive sins... [28] So the Son of Man is Lord even of the Sabbath."

"The phrase "Son of Man" or "son of Man" is found ninety-seven times in the book of Ezekiel and each time it refers to a human man. Arguably, in every instance of its use in the Old Testament it refers to a human or a man except for ***one time*** in the book of Daniel." **50.**

> Daniel 7:13-14 [13] "In my vision at night I looked, and there before me was one like *a son of man*, coming with the clouds of heaven. He approached the Ancient of Days and was led into his presence. [14] He was given authority, glory and

> sovereign power; all peoples, nations and men of every language worshiped him. His dominion is an everlasting dominion that will not pass away, and his kingdom is one that will never be destroyed."

"Here, in Daniel 7, son of man is an eternal being who is given power and authority as a god. It is from this one biblical source that a theology of messianic expectations was begun. It is not the only source found within the writings of the Second Temple Period, but perhaps the principal source.

Jesus adopted this term as the principal title that he would normally use to refer to himself. The term is used 78 times in the four Gospels. Almost every time, the words are attributed to the mouth of Jesus. Almost exclusively it is used in reference to his identifying with the work and mission of God's Messiah."

In Matthew 24:30 we read:

> [30] "At that time the sign of the Son of Man will appear in the sky, and all the nations of the earth will mourn. They will see the Son of Man coming on the clouds of the sky, with power and great glory."

It is Jesus who strikingly makes the connection between himself (Messiah) and Daniel's "son of man." In Matthew 24:37 we read further:

> ³⁷ "As it was in the days of Noah, so it will be at the coming of the Son of Man."

Here Jesus speaks of the coming of Messiah in the end times, a clarifying and prophetic word that there are two comings of Messiah, [a second coming].

In Matthew 9:6, the gospel records:

> ⁶ "But so that you may know that the Son of Man has authority on earth to forgive sins...." Then he said to the paralytic, "Get up, take your mat and go home."

Then he said to the paralytic, "Get up, take your mat and go home." In this passage Jesus is clearly proclaiming through action that He himself is the God when He refers to Messiah as the "Son of Man."

In John 13:31-32 we find another apostolic reading:

> ³¹ "When he was gone, Jesus said, "Now is the Son of Man glorified and God is glorified in him. ³² If God is glorified in

> him, God will glorify the Son in himself, and will glorify him at once."

This quotation from the lips of Jesus reveals to his disciples that he shares in God's glory as His Son.

"A final example is Luke 19:10. Here it reads:
> [10] "For the Son of Man came to seek and to save what was lost."

Jesus reaffirms that Messiah is God, for whom but God alone can save the lost?" [51].

The title Son of Man, as Jesus so often referred to himself, was not about his mortal life but his divine nature as God's Messiah. By using this title, Jesus clearly identifies himself to his hearers as divine!

NOTE: *This strongly refutes the false assumption that Jesus rarely admitted that he was the Son of God and God's Messiah.*

Both titles, the "Son of Man" and the "Son of God" at many times are interchangeable in their meaning and were titles that Jesus used to identify himself as the Messiah. These titles spoke of Messiah's mortality and they spoke of Messiah's divine nature. He would be fully human and fully God.

To some this was blasphemous.

"The objection of the scribes, calling Jesus' act of forgiveness "blasphemy," is predicated on their assumption that Jesus [who they knew to be a man] is claiming divinity through this action; hence their emphasis that only the *one* God may forgive sins, to which Jesus answers in kind: the second divine figure of Daniel 7, the one like a son of man, is authorized to act as and for God. This constitutes a direct declaration of a duality within the Godhead which is, of course, later on the very hallmark of Christian theology. [the Trinity]." **52.**

To others, it was the fulfillment of their expectant faith.

> Philippians 2:5-11 5 "Your attitude should be the same as that of Christ Jesus: 6 Who, being in very nature God, did not consider equality with God something to be grasped, 7 but made himself nothing, taking the very nature of a servant, being made in human likeness. 8 And being found in appearance as a man, he humbled himself and became obedient to death-- even death on a cross! 9 Therefore God

exalted him to the highest place and gave him the name that is above every name, [10] that at the name of Jesus every knee should bow, in heaven and on earth and under the earth, [11] and every tongue confess that Jesus Christ is Lord, to the glory of God the Father."

XI

The Godhead:
Messiah: Word, Logos and Wisdom

> John1:1-4 ¹"In the beginning was the Word, and the Word was with God, and the Word was God. ²He was with God in the beginning. ³Through him all things were made; without him nothing was made that has been made. ⁴In him was life, and that life was the light of men.

We start with a brief explanation of *Logos*. Logos is Greek for 'word'. John 1:1 translates all three instances of logos as 'the Word'. It is interesting to observe that Word, as it is used here, is capitalized. Why is that? In John, Word is someone's name!

Here in John's prologue, *Logos* has long been a Messianic title accepted by Christians without dissension. It needs to be correctly interpreted in both Christian and Jewish circles by understanding its origin and meaning. Interestingly, in the very readable Tyndale New Testament Commentaries on the Gospel of

John, R. V. G. Tasker, interestingly without ever mentioning the word "logos," attempts to connect its meaning through the use of Old Testament passages with the Hebrew word *dabhar* or *davar* which also means 'word'. [53]

While this interpretive understanding is acceptable, for our purposes we must make sure that we do not limit our understanding when speaking of the origin of meaning. Tasker rightly connects the Word, or Logos, with "a person being of and with God." [54]

In reference to the Hebrew word dabhar, Tasker wants us to understand that it is significant that dabhar is used both for word and for an event, and that this usage is found in both the Old and New Testaments. It would be beneficial for us to keep this following understanding in mind: Logos, Word, and Wisdom are interpreted simultaneously as nouns and verbs or nouns in action. As we review their historical interpretive usage, we should not disconnect the action from the title.

"It is the unique contribution of the prologue of the Gospel of John, that it reveals the Word of God not merely as an attribute of God, but as a distinct Person within the Godhead, dwelling with a creator before creation began, and acting as the divine agent in creation. The prologue speaks not of 'the word of God' but of *the Word* who *was with God and was God.*" [55.]

Tasker leaves unmentioned the origin of the term "logos" as being Greek, but quickly cites what he believes to be the Hebrew equivalent. What is not mentioned is that prior to the time of Jesus, a theology of the term logos existed. Allegory was the mode of interpretation concerning the logos. The concept of logos is that he is both the source of absolute creativity and the revealer of absolute truth. To promote allegory was a legitimate and choice mode of interpretation among Greeks. "Greek philosopher Origen, and his Jewish Alexandrian predecessor, Philo, both understood that a hermeneutic ungrounded in the "logos" was a source of disagreement among the Judeans." [56.]

"Born in different millennia from different ethnic cultures, Origen and Philo both see the

"Logos" as deeply embedded in the interpretive methods of the Judeans. A close examination of the Hebraic understanding of the various allegorical meanings of "Logos" is required. Messiah Son of David as King and anointed priest, along with the name Son of Man were names given to some of the agents of God's activity by the Judeans. "Logos" is one of these terms along with its related Aramaic equivalent *Memra* which is viewed as a divine agent." [57.]

"A major aspect of Jesus' ministry in the four Gospels is his preaching and teaching." [58.] "Logos/Memra" is the allegorical equivalent and fulfillment of the preaching, or proclamation, of God's Word by God's agent, or even by God Himself." [59.]

"To what extent the portrayal of him depends on anyone of the variety of Jewish and Gentile models is a point of considerable dispute. Our discussion of the Jewish text, however, suggest some possibilities that need to be investigated. Since the Gospels interpret Jesus's death with reference to the tradition of the persecuted spokesman of God, it is plausible that some of their descriptions of Jesus's preaching have also derived from the tradition. The accounts of Jesus' baptism are noteworthy in this respect, because the wording of a heavenly voice uses language from the Servant passage in Isaiah 42:1-2, and the stories serve as prologue to Jesus' Spirit – prompted ministry." **60.**

> 1 "Here is my servant, whom I uphold, my chosen one in whom I delight; I will put my Spirit on him and he will bring justice to the nations. 2 He will not shout or cry out or raise his voice in the streets. "

"The Hebraic understanding is that the "Logos/Memra" refers to the Word of God. Nickelsburg sees John 1:1-18 as probably quoting a Jewish exposition of Genesis 1:1-5 identifying Jesus as the preexistent Word (Logos/Memra) at the very beginning of John's Gospel.

> 1 "In the beginning God created the heavens and the earth. 2 Now the earth was formless and empty, darkness was over the surface of the deep, and the Spirit of God was hovering over the waters. 3 And God said, "Let there be

> light," and there was light. ⁴ God saw that the light was good, and he separated the light from the darkness. ⁵ God called the light "day," and the darkness he called "night." And there was evening, and there was morning-- the first day."

This Greek word (Logos) is seen to be endowed with a very Hebraic interpretive understanding. John's Gospel clearly connects the Logos/Word as being a divine other with God from the very beginning of creation, but existing before creation, because the Logos/Word was the creator. The Logos was the Word of God, meaning the one divine being known as the Logos/Word who spoke the word, or words of God.

John's allegorical connection of the Logos/Word and the spoken Word of God was that they were one (echad) and the same ('etzem). This way of thinking is within the understanding of the Hebraic interpretive methods used by Jesus, his disciples, and the Judeans of his time.

While this concept and interpretive approach, as placed within these terms, are foreign to the methods of Greco/Roman hermeneutics used by most Christians today. The Hebraic understanding is that Logos/Word/Memra was a name and title for the Divine Creator before His work of creation. The Word of God was this same divine being called the Logos. Additionally, this understanding reveals that the spoken Word of God brings wisdom. Wisdom was connected to the Word, just as Logos/Word/Memra are connected to all *being a name for God* and all *being God.*

The Hebraic understanding of Wisdom being divine is rooted in Proverbs 8:12-14, 22–23.

> [12] "I, wisdom, dwell together with prudence; I possess knowledge and discretion. [13] To fear the LORD is to hate evil; I hate pride and arrogance, evil behavior and perverse speech. [14] Counsel and sound judgment are mine; I have understanding and power.... [22] "The LORD brought me forth as the first of his works, before his deeds of old; [23] I

> was appointed from eternity, from the beginning, before the world began."

In the Old Testament and in other Second Temple Period Literature, "wisdom" is interpreted to be "a heavenly figure." [61.]

"That Jesus was thought to be the earthly presence of heavenly wisdom is attested to in several New Testament texts. Most briefly, it is stated in the hymns of Colossians 1:15–20.

> [15] "He is the image of the invisible God, the firstborn over all creation. [16] For by him all things were created: things in heaven and on earth, visible and invisible, whether thrones or powers or rulers or authorities; all things were created by him and for him. [17] He is before all things, and in him all things hold together. [18] And he is the head of the body, the church; he is the beginning and the firstborn from among the dead, so that in everything he might have the supremacy. [19] For God was pleased to have all his fullness dwell in him, [20] and

> through him to reconcile to himself all things, whether things on earth or things in heaven, by making peace through his blood, shed on the cross."

and Hebrews 1:1-4, both of which emphasize his role in creation." [62.]

> ¹ "In the past God spoke to our forefathers through the prophets at many times and in various ways, ² but in these last days he has spoken to us by his Son, whom he appointed heir of all things, and through whom he made the universe. ³ The Son is the radiance of God's glory and the exact representation of his being, sustaining all things by his powerful word. After he had provided purification for sins, he sat down at the right hand of the Majesty in heaven. ⁴ So he became as much superior to the angels as the name he has inherited is superior to theirs."

"The Johannine hymn to the Logos was inspired, (John 1:1–18) in content and in form, generally at least, in hymns about a more personified Wisdom, such as those in Proverbs 8 and Job 28:12–18". **63.**

> ¹² "But where can wisdom be found? Where does understanding dwell? ¹³ Man does not comprehend its worth; it cannot be found in the land of the living. ¹⁴ The deep says, 'It is not in me'; the sea says, 'It is not with me.' ¹⁵ It cannot be bought with the finest gold, nor can its price be weighed in silver. ¹⁶ It cannot be bought with the gold of Ophir, with precious onyx or sapphires. ¹⁷ Neither gold nor crystal can compare with it, nor can it be had for jewels of gold. ¹⁸ Coral and jasper are not worthy of mention; the price of wisdom is beyond rubies."

"Logos was Word. Word was Wisdom and Wisdom was God. God dwelt in heaven. Logos, therefore, in the thoughts of Judeans, dwelt in the heavens. It follows that when John wrote his Gospel and declared, "In the beginning was the Word – Logos, the Judeans of his time understood that John was calling Jesus the divine God who lived in heaven and was the creator of all things." **64.**

"In the first and second centuries, there were Jewish non-Christians who firmly held theological doctrines of the second God, variously called Logos, Memra. Sophia or Wisdom,...; indeed, perhaps *most of the Jews* did so at the time." **65.**

"The understanding of a 'complexity within the Godhead' preexisted the time of Jesus within Judean faith. The Logos, or second person in the Godhead, was known by several names, including the Aramaic term Memra, the Greek term Sophia, or Wisdom, among others. 'In the early centuries were non-Christian Jews who believed in God's Word, Wisdom, or even a *Son* as a "second God'." **66.**

"The literary evidence, before and after the incarnation of Jesus, speaks of a rich theological foundation of belief that God either existed as being more than one in Himself, or that there was more than one God in heaven. John applies the term Logos (Word) to Jesus. This richly interpreted Hebraic title calls Jesus the pre-existent Divine Creator. The word Logos may be Greek, but its meaning is interpretively Hebraic. Jesus would draw from this rich Second Temple Period interpretive environment and give clarity to those ideas that more accurately reflect His person, nature and calling. In John chapter 1 verse 18, the apostle writes in His Gospel; 'No one has ever seen God, but God the one and only, who is at the Father's side, has made Him known"." **67.**

> John 1:1-18 [1] "In the beginning was the Word, and the Word was with God, and the Word was God. [2] He was with God in the beginning. [3] Through him all things were made; without him nothing was made that has been made. [4] In him was life, and that life was the light of men. [5] The light shines in the darkness, but the darkness has not understood it. [6] There came a man who was sent from God; his name was John. [7] He came as a witness to testify concerning that light, so that through him all men might believe. [8] He himself was not the light; he came only as a witness to the light. [9] The true light

that gives light to every man was coming into the world. ¹⁰ He was in the world, and though the world was made through him, the world did not recognize him. ¹¹ He came to that which was his own, but his own did not receive him. ¹² Yet to all who received him, to those who believed in his name, he gave the right to become children of God-- ¹³ children born not of natural descent, nor of human decision or a husband's will, but born of God. ¹⁴ The Word became flesh and made his dwelling among us. We have seen his glory, the glory of the One and Only, who came from the Father, full of grace and truth. ¹⁵ John testifies concerning him. He cries out, saying, "This was he of whom I said, 'He who comes after me has surpassed me because he was before me.'" ¹⁶ From the fullness of his grace we have all received one blessing after another. ¹⁷ For the law was given through Moses; grace and truth came through Jesus Christ. ¹⁸ No one has ever seen God, but God the One and Only, who is at the Father's side, has made him known."

XII

The Godhead:
Messiah - Immanuel

"All of the ideas about Christ [Messiah] are old; the new is Jesus [the man]. There is nothing in the doctrine of the Christ [Messiah] that is new save the declaration of this man as the Son of Man. This is, of course, an enormous declaration, a huge innovation in itself and one that has had fateful historical consequences." **68.**

Let us begin by defining a particular Hebrew word. This Hebrew word is one that most Christians should be familiar. It is the word "Immanuel" which literally means "with us (is) God." We reverse it in English and say, "God with us."

Immanuel is used only twice in the Old Testament and both times it is used as a proper name.

> Isaiah 7:14 "Therefore the Lord himself will give you a sign: The virgin will be with child and will give birth to a son and will call him ***Immanuel***."

> Isaiah 8:8 "and sweep on into Judah, swirling over it, passing through it and reaching up to the neck. Its outspread wings will cover the breadth of your land, **O Immanuel!**"

As we look into the interpretive idea of "God with us" we want to bring a focus upon the purpose behind his coming as a man. Isaiah 7:14 is the text from which we draw our interpretive understanding that Immanuel is a name for Messiah.

One Given Authority

We move forward in the book of Isaiah to discover another fascinating passage of Scripture that also speaks directly of child, a son to be exact, who would be borne and have a tremendous impact upon mankind. That passage is Isaiah 9:6.

> "For to us a child is born, to us a son is given, and the government will be on his shoulders. And he will be called Wonderful Counselor, Mighty God, Everlasting Father, Prince of Peace."

We see a direct connection between "Immanuel" of Isaiah 7:14 and the "child" who is a "son" in Isaiah 9:6 to be one and the same person. It is not Ahaz or one of his offspring because the verse doesn't speak of a normal birth. In Isaiah 7:14 the son who is to be called "Immanuel" is born of a virgin. This is a declaration that the offspring is not the product of human seed, but of supernatural seed. For the "child" (son) who is born, the one given, is divine. We know this because He will be called "Mighty God, Everlasting Father". Clearly this "*son*" is a supernatural other, He is God.

Both of these passages in Isaiah are principal texts that move us toward an understanding that a "son" is to be born supernaturally. But they are not the primary sources for our expectation of such a promise. We may ask "What text sets up our expectancy of "God being with us"? Where do we find the beginning for our understanding that God Himself would become a man and dwell among us? That principal passage is Genesis 3:15.

> [15] "And I will put enmity between you and the woman, and between your offspring and hers; he will crush your head, and you will strike his heel."

Most of the scriptures I use are quoted from the New International Version but in this case it isn't as true to the Hebrew it translates. So, we are inclined to reference the King James Version.

> **KJV** Genesis 3:15 "And I will put enmity between thee and the woman, and between thy seed and her seed; it shall bruise thy head, and thou shalt bruise his heel."

We need to first state and then reflect upon the peculiar statement concerning a woman and her "seed." The New International Version translates the Hebrew word for "seed" as "offspring" which can dilute the interpretive strength of this Hebrew verse. The Hebrew word for "seed" is "zerah" from which we get the proper name Sarah. In this verse 'zerah' is singular. The serpent is understood to have a "seed" and the woman is understood to have a "seed". Without being too surprised by the wording we can begin to consider the meaning of the serpent's "seed", but we do a little more head scratching when we try to consider the thought of a woman having "seed".

To be direct, women biologically do not have seed. So, what could possibly be meant by "her seed"? Interpretively, the groundwork for a future virgin birth is set in place. It is impossible for a woman to conceive and to become pregnant, on her own. In Hebrew thought, the only possible way for a virgin to become pregnant was by supernatural means. It was therefore expected that God would be the father of a virgin's baby. The life from the woman would make the child human and the supernatural seed implanted within her by God would make the child divine. Not only would the child be both human and divine, the child would more specifically be a male, a "son" and he would be called "Immanuel", "God with us".

Keeping these thoughts in mind let's look at a New Testament passage that is a part of John the Disciple's very unique birth narrative. In chapter seven we spoke more in-depth about the revelation that Messiah would also be known as the "Word". John's reflection was that this much anticipated baby that would be born of a virgin would most definitely be God himself and be called the "Word". In John's narrative he doesn't mention a baby being born to the virgin Mary as does Matthew and Luke, but Matthew specifically calls the baby "Immanuel".

> Matthew 1:20-23   [20] "But after he had considered this, an angel of the Lord appeared to him in a dream and said, "Joseph son of David, do not be afraid to take Mary home as your wife, because what is conceived in her is from the Holy Spirit. [21] She will give birth to a son, and you are to give him the name Jesus, because he will save his people from their sins." [22] All this took place to fulfill what the Lord had said through the prophet: [23] "The virgin will be with child and will give birth to a son, and they will

call him *Immanuel*"--which means, "God with us."

Matthew gives a wonderful summation of the Hebraically derived Messianic understanding of the birth of God's son which was taken from passages that we have looked at from Genesis and Isaiah. To Matthew, Jesus was born of a virgin and was Messiah, God!

And in his own unique way John does the same in the first chapter of his gospel. Here is John's summation in verse 14:

> John 1:14 "The Word became flesh and made his dwelling among us. We have seen his glory, the glory of the One and Only, who came from the Father, full of grace and truth."

John, who seems to have taken the best of all three verses from Matthew 1, has given us his condensed version. The Word (who is God Messiah) became flesh (born in human form, a son) who made his dwelling among us (a gift given to mankind) and the result is that we have seen His glory (intimate, personal revelation, illumination and presence) the one and only (singular in appearing) who came from the Father (supernatural seed) full of grace and truth (came in love).

NOTE: ""dwelling among" is a translation of the Greek word *ska-noo*. It is the verb form of the noun *ske-ne* and both mean *live, dwell,* and *to tabernacle.*"

Ske-ne is used in the Greek text of the Old Testament (Septuagint) and is the translation for the Hebrew word *Mishkan*. Mishkan was the honored name for the Tent of Meeting that Moses set up in the wilderness for the people to meet with and worship God. This specific word, chosen by John, is not by mistake and directs us to consider something more. Something more than what 'God lived and made his dwelling among us' means.

In light of the purpose of the Mishkan which Moses set up in the desert, we are able to consider the idea that "to tabernacle" means that Immanuel has come to offer the same depth of "spiritual communion" to us as He did when His presence dwelt over the tabernacle in the wilderness. Immanuel just didn't merely show himself to us, he came to live/commune with us.

There is a central purpose in discussing our understanding of Immanuel; it is something that we must not neglect. And for that we return to Genesis 3:15 for a closer look. The statement "And I will put enmity" is a curious choice of words found at the beginning of this verse and sets up the intended conclusion delivered at the end of the verse. We begin to see that the actions of God, which will culminate in the birth of a son by a virgin, has more to it than just being a spectacular supernatural achievement. While the birth of a child should always be a happy and exhilarating experience, the purpose for this child's coming is undoubtedly attached to this statement: "I will put *enmity* between you and the woman..."

If we were to review all of the popular English translations of this passage, we would find that they all translate this portion of the passage with the same words, "and I will put enmity between you and the woman." The Hebrew is just that straightforward with the keyword being "enmity." Please do not mistake the structure and meaning of this word. It is not a verb; *it is a noun*. Here *enmity* is not an action or an emotional feeling that comes between the serpent and the woman. No, it refers to a person! It is the *woman's seed*!

The Hebrew for our English word *enmity* is quite a fascinating study. The first part of the compound word means *Woe*. The second part means "house," and since it is singular it literally means "a house of woe!". If we could put this idea into a single noun it would be "enemy." Let us insert the word 'enemy' into this verse. "And I will put an *enemy* between you and the woman." Pretty clear and straight forward. But whose enemy is it? The woman's? No. The serpent's! Messiah will stand between the woman and the serpent.

Let us look at one more thing from this verse that needs clarification. Who is the serpent? While ancient sages understood that the Messiah will step on the head of the snake and defeat evil once and for all, they also understood the snake to be Satan. "At first glance, it is difficult to see this verse as a

Messianic prophecy. The Targumim [Aramaic translations of the Old Testament], however, which are so important to our early Jewish understanding of the Scriptures, relate this particular verse to the Messiah and his battle against HaSatan [the Satan]." [69] "The Torah establishes this message, explaining that the Messiah is to appear in order to defeat HaSatan once and for all. ...Only through the Messiah can one overcome HaSatan according to Torah. [Genesis through Deuteronomy]" [70]

And the New Testament agrees.

> 1 John 3:8 "He who does what is sinful is of the devil [Satan], because the devil has been sinning from the beginning. The reason the Son of God appeared was to destroy the devil's work."

God ordained that the restoration of mankind to himself would require that he place an "enemy" between Satan and the woman. And this enemy of Satan would come with _hostile intentions_ toward the one who had tempted the woman to fall into sin.

Now keep this scenario in the forefront of your mind as we project our thoughts from Genesis four thousand years into the future. And from our present time, project ourselves two thousand years into the past. We are transported to a comely pastoral scene surrounding the birth of Immanuel. Angels are singing in the heavens and shepherds are bowing in worship near a manger where the newborn Son of God rests. But we now instantly fly away from this tranquil earthly moment and are transported into a heavenly spiritual realm where a thunderous declaration of war has just been given. Satan's worst nightmare has just entered the arena of men. The battle is on!

Our study does not end here. John declared that Satan has been sinning since the beginning, and in another Scripture, we are told a third of heaven fell into sin with him. When Satan tempted Adam and Eve causing them to sin against God, it was because of their sin he usurped the authority over death and hell (i.e., judgment). Mankind became recipients of his judgment. He became their chief accuser.

God, however, had a plan. The purposed outcome for the life of Immanuel, as the enemy of Satan, was to restore to God *all authority* over death and hell. By restoring this authority to himself, he was fully justified to forgive all the sins of mankind, restore them to a righteous relationship with himself and condemn Satan and his fallen angels to a fiery judgment.

A common understanding of "Immanuel, God with us" is this: "God who is now with us." But there is more to it than having God with us. Let us therefore place the emphasis back upon GOD! Immanuel came to undo all the works of Satan and in doing so he took back the authority to rule his creation!

> Psalm 110:1 "...The LORD says to my Lord: "Sit at my right hand until I make your enemies a footstool for your feet."

> Hebrews 10:5-13 5 "Therefore, when Christ came into the world, he said: "Sacrifice and offering you did not desire, but a body you prepared for me; 6 with burnt offerings and sin offerings you

were not pleased. ⁷ Then I said, 'Here I am-- it is written about me in the scroll-- I have come to do your will, O God.'" ⁸ First he said, "Sacrifices and offerings, burnt offerings and sin offerings you did not desire, nor were you pleased with them" (although the law required them to be made). ⁹ Then he said, "Here I am, I have come to do your will." He sets aside the first to establish the second. ¹⁰ And by that will, we have been made holy through the sacrifice of the body of Jesus Christ once for all. ¹¹ Day after day every priest stands and performs his religious duties; again and again he offers the same sacrifices, which can never take away sins. ¹² But when this priest had offered for all time one sacrifice for sins, he sat down at the right hand of God. ¹³ Since that time he waits for his enemies to be made his footstool,"

Jude 1:24 ²⁴ "To him who is able to keep you from falling and to present you before his glorious presence without fault and with great joy-- ²⁵ to the only

God our Savior be glory, majesty, power and authority, through Jesus Christ our Lord, before all ages, now and forevermore! Amen."

Messiah/Immanuel will be a *house of woe* to HaSatan, (the satan)!

Messiah *will undo* all the evil that Satan has done to man!

XIII

The Godhead: The Holy Spirit

"The Holy Spirit is God's gift of Himself to His creation." (Cairns, 2019)

> Psalm 51:11 "Do not cast me from your presence or take your Holy Spirit from me."

Let us continue our sacred journey with the discovery of who the Holy Spirit is by defining our terms from the Biblical Hebrew. "The holy spirit" is the conventional translation of the Hebrew phrase "ruah ha-kodesh." [71.] "Ha-kodesh" is the Hebrew for "the holy." It represents those people, places and things that are separated unto, and dedicated to God. It is also an attribute of God, meaning God is "holy". Being "holy", we understand that the Spirit of God is totally set apart to perform the will of God. He is entirely pure in His motives. He is morally good and perfect, and His actions are never at odds with those of the Father and/or the Son.

"Ruah" (pronounced "rue-ack") is the Hebrew word for *"breath, wind or spirit"*. When "ruah" is used within the Hebrew text, we need to examine the context to assist us in determining the most suitable English word that closely identifies with the action being described. What is interesting is that all three of these defining words apply quite fittingly to our understanding of God's "spirit". It is from these three words, *breath, wind, spirit*, that we can formulate a working understanding of the Spirit of God.

Like many Hebrew words, "breath, wind, and spirit" can function as both verbs and nouns, depending upon the context in which they are used. What they mutually hold in common is the phenomenon of being observed or recognized *only when they are in motion.*

Breath (Heb. neshamah) is the air contained within our lungs, but it can also mean the action of exhaling. Taking a breathe is to inhale, but to breath (neshamah) is to inhale and then to exhale or blow wind out of the lungs. When the air temperature is a little bit colder, we can literally see our breath as we exhale.

Wind in action, as in the skies, is only observed when clouds are pushed across the vast expanse of the heavens or when it causes the rustling of leaves on tree branches or causes the grass in the fields to sway.

Spirit may be an attribute of a human being or an animal, but, like our breath and the wind, it is never observed and confirmed until it is in motion. From this we can claim an ability to recognize and speak about the attributes of the *ruah hakodesh, Holy Spirit.* However, we can and do apply such specific understanding of the Holy Spirit when He is in motion. Yes, it may be said that the Holy Spirit rests upon someone but even when He is resting, He remains in motion! Meaning, He is always "at work."

What may be surprising for many is that the Spirit of God is one of the most revealed truths found in Scripture. Spirit of God, Spirit of the Lord, and The Holy Spirit are all names which refer to the same person. When we want to be more personal, we do not use a title, but the name 'Holy Spirit'.

Some confusion comes, however, when we stop to consider the person, character, and nature of the Holy Spirit, and recognize this one amazing fact; His actions are never done for the purpose of directly revealing Himself. It is not that He is attempting to hide Himself from us. It is because self-revelation is not His primary mission. He is always acting on behalf of another, that is, the Father or the Son. He is either imparting Himself into someone or something, or He is impacting someone or something. In all cases we can be assured that the Holy Spirit's purpose is always good, even while His purposes may remain a mystery or His ways are misunderstood by us.

The Godhead: A Trinity

If we are to interpretively declare that the Holy Spirit is the third person in the Godhead, along with the Father and the Son, we are undoubtedly making a distinction between the three. Although we agree with Deuteronomy 6:4 (The Shema) that there is only *one God* who is wholly unified in His being, and yet God exists as three.

If this is true then we are able to look for those particular attributes that would individually define these three persons who somehow exist in, and as, one Being. They are united as "one", yet we are calling them by different names thereby recognizing three distinct persons in one Being.

We have described their unity, but how do we distinguish their 'separateness' ? A distinction that we can use to describe the unique union of Father, Son, and Holy Spirit would be their "purpose" or "work".

Their character and nature are exactly the same. They are equally holy, loving, and gracious. They exist as heavenly spirit. Their purposes are always carried out in harmony to bring about their agreed-upon goals. And They think the same, or to put it another way, They are united in Their thinking.

NOTE: When I state that They think the same, I am not trying to insinuate that what each of Them thinks is simultaneously thought or known totally by the other two. There does seem to be some independence within Their thinking and in Their behavior. But this does not indicate that Their independent thinking and behavior are in any way opposed to or contrary to the thoughts and behavior of each other.

The evidence of scripture is that They are totally united to bring about mutually desired outcomes and are never to be considered as working independently of each other.

Scripture gives us a very strong indication that these last few statements are true.

> Genesis 1:26 26"Then God said, 'Let us make man in our image, in our likeness, and let them rule over the fish of the sea and the birds of the air, over the livestock, over all the earth, and over all the creatures that move along the ground.' "

If we examine the life of Messiah, while He was in earthly form, He waited for the Father to reveal His thoughts and purposes without becoming a puppet.

> John 8:28 28 "So Jesus said, 'When you have lifted up the Son of Man, then you will know that I am *the one I claim to be* and that I do nothing on my own but

> speak just what the Father has taught me.'"
>
> John 10:37 ³⁷ "Do not believe me unless I do what my Father does."

It is also clear that Messiah only did the will of the Father through the power of the Holy Spirit!

> John 1:32-33 ³² "Then John gave this testimony: 'I saw the Spirit come down from heaven as a dove and remain on him. ³³ I would not have known him, except that the one who sent me to baptize with water told me, 'The man on whom you see the Spirit come down and remain is he who will baptize with the Holy Spirit.'"
>
> Luke 4:1 ¹ "Jesus, full of the Holy Spirit, returned from the Jordan and was led by the Spirit in the desert,"
>
> Matthew 12:28 ²⁸ "But if I drive out demons by the Spirit of God, then the kingdom of God has come upon you."

Furthermore, we see that there was some degree of knowledge that only the Father had, and when it was appropriate, he would reveal it to his Son.

> Mark 13:32 [32] "No one knows about that day or hour, not even the angels in heaven, nor the Son, but only the Father."

Our ability to interpretively discover the truth about a Divine Father and a Divine Son is challenging but not impossible. Christianity, and the ancient Judeans who lived prior to the coming of Messiah, had concluded from their interpretive discovery that the Divine Father and Divine Son were both part of the same Godhead.

What can we say then about the Holy Spirit? Is He a third person in the Godhead? What we begin to discover is that after the time of Messiah, the understanding of the Holy Spirit began to go through a time of interpretive adjustments, both within Christianity and Rabbinical Judaism.

Within rabbinical writings about the Holy Spirit, which at one time was thought and taught to be pervasive in all divine activity, we observe that the rabbis began to reduce the activity of the Holy Spirit to a significantly smaller circle of human agents.

This adjusted teaching did not always attract the majority opinion. Concerning the *Ruah ha-kodesh* [the Holy Spirit], we began to see divergent interpretive developments of this concept. This was and is observed between rabbinic teaching and Christian theology, where many variations of meaning have emerged. Yet what we do agree upon is quite surprising and at times <u>it is surprising about how much we do agree!</u>

Rabbi Dr. Aaron Singer writes from a Jewish veiwpoint: "The term *Ruah ha-kodesh* turns on the axis of God's self-revelation to man. Whatever the philological origins [whatever was originally concluded from interpretively studying this Hebrew term] *ruah ha-kodesh* has come to signify a prophetic spirit that graces an individual or community.

The bearer experiences a clairvoyance [a clearer understanding of things] that enables him to discern an event or human encounter in the continuum of time and space, illuminate the text of the Torah [all scripture is implied], be inspired to transcribe a book of Scripture, and, in some cases, perform supernatural feats.

Ruah ha-kodesh also manifests itself [Rabbinical Judaism does not call *ruah ha-kodesh* He or Him] as a personification of the holy writ [Word], or as a divine epithet [added meaning to someone, i.e. I AM Whom I AM]. In this capacity, *ruah ha-kodesh* quotes Scripture to admonish, comfort, and guide Israel [and if Israel, then all believers]. The Holy Spirit and the dogma [established teachings] of the early church becomes a coeternal hypostasis [equally eternal and supportive foundation] in the doctrine of the Trinity. *Ruah ha-kodesh,* on the other hand, is a didactic dramatization [exampled teaching] of God's immediacy and not a substantial intermediary between God and man." [72.]

It is interesting to note that even "in rabbinic literature, *ruah ha-kodesh* plays an active role in the haggadahic narrative [telling or instructional teaching] of the Bible. The prophetic spirit supplies Adam with names to give to the creatures God has created; appears in the courts of Shem, Samuel, and Solomon; advises Sarah; enlightens Jacob as to the future of his sons; flees from Moses due to the unworthiness of the Israel that worshiped the golden calf; and inspires David and Solomon to compose the books of Psalms and Ecclesiastes, respectively. *Ruah ha-kodesh* is attributed to 48 men and seven women of the Bible [OT], and it was thought that *ruah ha-kodesh* was abundant in Israel before the disappearance of Elijah." [73.]

"*Ruah ha-kodesh* is responsible for all degrees of prophecy;" [74.] with the interpretation of Holy Scripture being of the highest order. Under the power of the Holy Spirit the biblical "prophet is compelled to admonish Israel for its sins and call for repentance before it is too late. He is often caught between the fire of his divine mission and his love of Israel. When tragedy and despair overwhelmed Israel, he comforts it with messianic visions of better days. In contrast the non-biblical [actions of the Holy Spirit not recorded in the Bible] *ruah ha-kodesh* falls like a gentle rain rather than a cataclysmic whirlwind on its recipient. [It can be] ...merely an experience of illumination, a feeling of exultation.

Like other forms of theophany in rabbinic teaching, *ruah ha-kodesh* is associated with man's religious and moral behavior. *Ruah ha-kodesh* is a gift, not a burden, that is linked to performing a mizvah (religious precept such as water baptism) or living an exemplary life. Further, the experience of *ruah ha-kodesh* enables the righteous to enlarge the circle [influence] of his righteousness," [75].

"We have seen in Torah that God's Spirit helped birth the world, bring humanity to life, and give humans understanding of God and the purpose of our existence. In the dimension of creation, we feel God's spirit within us as we breathe, keeping us alive, giving us a connection to the source of our lives. In the dimension of revelation, we feel God's spirit as inspiration as we move from existence, to awareness, to insight, to a sense of purpose. God's spirit opens a line of communication between humanity and the divine, enabling human beings to understand how we are to live and to contribute ourselves to our world. The dimension of redemption is fueled by our aspirations for wholeness. We exist, we understand, and therefore we strive. Alive and awake, we find ourselves in a partnership with God with a shared imperative -- to heal and repair our world. It is not enough to breathe. It is not enough to feel inspired by miracles and seek wisdom. We cannot be satisfied." [76.]

We have only just begun our search for an understanding of the Holy Spirit. There is so much more to be said and even so much more to be experienced. But let us close out this chapter by taking a short tour through Scripture to give us an introductory glimpse of the purpose and work of the third person in the Godhead.

The Holy Spirit is:
Presence:

John 1:32-33 ³² "Then John gave this testimony: 'I saw the Spirit come down from heaven as a dove and remain on him...' "

Salvation:

Acts 19:2 ² "Did you receive the Holy Spirit when you believed?"

Power:

Acts 19:6 ⁶ "When Paul placed his hands on them, the Holy Spirit came on them, and they spoke in tongues and prophesied."

To Be Respected:

Job 27:1-4 ¹ "And Job continued his discourse: 'As surely as God lives, who has denied me justice, the Almighty, who has made me taste bitterness of soul, ³as long as I have life within me, the breath of God in my nostrils, ⁴my lips will not speak wickedness, and my tongue will utter no deceit.' "

Mark 3:29 ²⁹ "But whoever blasphemes against the Holy Spirit will never be forgiven; he is guilty of an eternal sin."

Justice:

> Isaiah 42:1 "Behold My Servant, whom I uphold, My chosen, in whom My Soul delights: I have put My Spirit upon him, he will bring forth justice to the nations."

> Isaiah 63:10 [10] "Yet they rebelled and grieved his Holy Spirit. So he turned and became their enemy and he himself fought against them."

Life Giving:

> Genesis 1:2 [2] "Now the earth was formless and empty, darkness was over the surface of the deep, and the Spirit of God was hovering over the waters."

> Job 33:4 [4] "The Spirit of God has made me; the breath of the Almighty gives me life."

Indwelling:

Genesis 41:38 ³⁸ "So Pharaoh asked them, 'Can we find anyone like this man, one in whom is the spirit of God?' "

Anointing our Skills:

Exodus 31:3 ³ "and I have filled him with the Spirit of God, with skill, ability and knowledge in all kinds of crafts—"

Habitation:

Isaiah 63:11 ¹¹ "Then his people recalled the days of old, the days of Moses and his people--where is he who brought them through the sea, with the shepherd of his flock? Where is he who set his Holy Spirit among them,"

Prophetic Spirit:

1 Samuel 10:9-10 ⁹ "As Saul turned to leave Samuel, God changed Saul's heart, and all these signs were fulfilled that day. ¹⁰When they arrived at Gibeah, a procession of prophets met him; the

Spirit of God came upon him in power, and he joined in their prophesying."

Amos 3:8 ⁸ "The lion has roared--who will not fear? The Sovereign LORD has spoken--who can but prophesy?"

Counselor:
John 14:16 ¹⁶ "And I will ask the Father, and he will give you another Counselor to be with you forever—"
Truth:
John 14:17 ¹⁷ "the Spirit of truth..."
Rejected: (as Messiah being rejected)
John 14:17 ¹⁷ "...The world cannot accept him, because it neither sees him nor knows him..."
Abiding in you:
John 14:17 "...But you know him, for he lives with you and will be in you."

The Holy Spirit is the third person in the Trinity.

XIV

Closing Thoughts

The Jesus Reclamation Project is a field of study being undertaken by Jewish scholars beginning as early as the 1960s. Leaders in these studies include David Flusser, Pinchas Lapide, Geza Vermes, Mark Nanos, Amy Jill-Levine and Daniel Boyarin, among others. Their studies and publications advanced their position that Jesus was historically and authentically Judean (the proper term other than Jewish) as evidenced in his teachings and ministry.

Another field of study, yet un-named, could be The Judaism Reclamation Project. Jewish leaders in this recovery project are Neil Gillman, Arthur Cohen, Paul Mendes-Flohr, Louis Jacobs and Aaron Singer among many including some of those listed above. Their studies focus upon the re-discovery, reclamation and perhaps re-establishment of the Biblically formed ancient foundational beliefs of the Jewish people. They believe these ancient beliefs are needed to justify and support their behavioral practices as people of the book.

These projects just so happen to coincide with a project that I and other believers in Messiah are currently engaged. This Messianic project is aimed at reclaiming and repositioning Jesus as the Jewish Messiah. Tied in with this project are studies that are also reclaiming the origins of our Biblical doctrines.

Current findings are that the doctrines ascribed to Messiah and His teachings originated prior to Messiah Immanuel and within the faith of the ancient Judeans. The material source for these doctrines, also was the Old Testament as well. The paths of our research and our theological conclusions converge with many of the Jewish scholars if we mutually begin at the time of Jesus and backward to the time of the Patriarchs (Genesis – Deuteronomy or Torah).

Judean faith was not only the primary belief system of the Jews at that time, but it was **the belief system** held by the majority of Jews and the belief system held by Jesus and His disciples.

This book, and its predecessor, Sacred Journey I, employed these methods to reclaim our beliefs where necessary, and re-establish and re-affirm them when neglected. That which once was known, accepted and practiced, we still believe!

It is apparent that too many generations of modern believers in Jesus have forgotten that their beliefs have deep roots and are grounded in powerful truth statements that are defendable against all challenges. My prayer is that by knowing how consistent and established these truths are, this knowledge will strengthen your convictions in the revelations of scripture and lead you into a deeper place of faith and trust in our Messiah.

__Finding Salvation on the Roman Road__

1. *Recognize and confess that you are a sinner*

    Romans 3:23 "for all have sinned and fall short of the glory of God,"

2. *The penalty of sin is eternal death*

    Romans 6:23 "For the wages of sin is death,

3. *Jesus has paid the penalty and offers you life eternal with Him*

    ... but the gift of God is eternal life in Christ Jesus our Lord."

4. *Ask Jesus to forgive your sin and unbelief and save you.*

    Romans 10:13 "for, 'Everyone who calls on the name of the Lord will be saved.'"

5. *Why not NOW!*

Revelation 3:20 "Here I am! I stand at the door and knock. If anyone hears my voice and opens the door, I will come in and eat with him, and he with me."

ENDNOTES

1. Louis Jacobs. "Faith". *Contemporary Jewish Religious Thought.* Artur A. Cohen & Paul Mendes-Flohr eds.. The Free Press: New York, 1988. 234.

2. Ibid., 233.

3. Ibid.

4. Myer Pearlman. *Knowing the Doctrines of the Bible.* Springfield. MO.: Gospel Publishing House, 1981. 33.

5. Ibid., op. cit., "God". *Contemporary Jewish Religious Thought.* 291.

6. Ibid., 292.

7. Myer Perlman. *Knowing the Doctrines of the Bible.* The Gospel Publishing House: Springfield, 1981. 35.

8. Ibid., op. cit., *Contemporary Jewish Thought.* 291.

9. Ibid., 292.

10. Ibid.

11. https://www.blueletterbible.org/faq/don_stewart/don_stewart_377.cfm

12. https://www.britannica.com/biography/Antony-Flew. English Philosopher, written by Matt Stefon (as of 9/2019)

13. http://www.cslewis.com/a-note-on-the-socratic-club/ (as of 9/2019)

14. https://www.cslewisinstitute.org/node/46 *"University Battles: CS Lewis and the Oxford University Socratic Club"* by Christopher W Mitchell. (Published in *C.S. Lewis: Lightbearer in the Shadowlands*, Edited by Angus Menuge, Crossway Books, 1997. 329-352

15. Justin Phillips. *CS Lewis: In a Time of War.* Harper Collins: 2002. 303 – 307.

16. Ibid.

17. Neil Gillman. *The Jewish Approach to God: A Brief Introduction for Christians.* "God

is Echad." Woodstock: Jewish Lights, 201.) 1.

18. Ibid., 1-2.

19. Ibid., 2.

20. Ibid.

21. Ibid., 10.

22. https://www.myjewishlearning.com/article/can-god-be-our-king-and-our-parent/ by Hanan Schlesinger (as of 5/2020)

23. Daniel Boyarin. *The Jewish Gospels. The Story of the Jewish Christ.* New York: The New Press, 2012. 4.
24. Ibid., 5.

25. John K Cairns Jr.. *Scared Journey Vol. I. Finding God in our Pursuit of Truth, Knowledge, God Culture and the Meaning of Life.* The Source of Knowledge III. Wayne NJ: Metro Jewish Resources, 2020. 55.

26. Mark Boda and Gordon McConville. eds, *Messiah Dictionary of the Old Testament*

Prophets. Downers Grove: IVP Academic, 2012. 537.

27. David B Levenson. *The Jewish Annotated New Testament. Messianic Movements.* Amy-Jill Levine & Marc Zvi Brettler eds. Oxford: University Press, 2011. 531.

28. David Flusser. *Judaism and the Origins of Christianity.* (Jerusalem. The Magnes Press. 1988) 424.

29. Israel Jacob Yuval. Two Nations in Your Womb. *Perceptions of Jews and Christians in Late Antiquity and the Middle Ages.* (Berkeley. University of California. 2006) 35.

30. Boda. 539.

31. Ibid.

32. Flusser. 423-424.

33. Ibid., 424-425.

34. David Klinghoffer. *Why the Jews Rejected Jesus.* (New York. Random House, 2005) 79.

35. Levenson. 531.

36. Ibid. 535.

37. Boyarin. 130.

38. Ibid., 131.

39. Ibid. 132-133.

40. Arnold G. Fruchtenbaum. *Jesus was a Jew*. San Antonio: Ariel Ministries, 2010. 15–24.

41. Boyarin. 25-26.

42. Ibid. 25-26.

43. Ibid. 26.

44. George W.E. Nickelsburg *Ancient Judaism and Christian Origins. Diversity, Continuity and Transformation.* Minneapolis: Fortress Press, 2003. 89-90

45. Boyarin. 27–28.

46. Ibid., 28-29.

47. Ibid., 30.

48. Ibid.

49. Ibid. 31.

50. John K Cairns Jr.. *Hebraic Studies that Present a Striking Case for Reimaging the Origin of the Faith and Teachings of Jesus.* (Doctoral Project. 2013) 67.

51. Ibid. 67-69.

52. Boyarin. 58.

53. R.V.G. Tasker. *John: Tyndall New Testament Commentaries.* Grand Rapids: William B Erdman's Publishing Company, 1988. 41.

54. Ibid., 42.

55. Ibid.

56. Daniel Boyarin. "Philo, Origen, and the Rabbis on Divine Speech and Interpretation." in *The World of Early Egyptian Christianity: Essays in Honor of David W. Johnson.* James E Goebring and Janet A. Timbie, eds., Washington: The

Catholic University of America Press, 2007. 113.

57. Cairns. 71.

58. Nickelsburg, 112.

59. Cairns. 71.

60. Nickelsburg. 112.

61. Cairns. 72-73.

62. Nickelsburg, 104.

63. Ibid., 113.

64. Cairns. 73.

65. Daniel Boyarin. *Border Lines: The Partition of Judeo-Christianity.* Philadelphia. University of Pennsylvania Press, 2004. 92.

66. Ibid. 90.

67. Cairns. 74.

68. Boyarin. *The Jewish Gospels.* 101.

69. Itzhak Shapiro. *The Return of the Kosher Pig: The Divine Messiah in Jewish Thought.* Clarksville: Lederer Books, 2013. 122.

70. Ibid., 178.

71. Aaron Singer. "Holy Spirit" in *Contemporary Jewish Religious Thought.* Arthur A. Cohen and Paul Mendes-Flohr eds. New York: The Free Press, 1987. 409.

72. Ibid., 409-410.

73. Ibid.

74. Ibid.

75. Ibid.

76. Rachel Timoner. *Breath of Life: God as Spirit in Judaism.* Brewster: Paraclete Press, 2011. 97.

www.ingramcontent.com/pod-product-compliance
Lightning Source LLC
Chambersburg PA
CBHW071400290426
44108CB00014B/1622